Blossoming
through
Adversity

Blossoming through Adversity

Unveiling the Power of Post-Traumatic Growth and the Ecstasy of Exploration

by Melissa Triano

Won't Stay Quiet

Copyright © 2023 Melissa Triano
All rights reserved

No part of this book or e-book may be used or reproduced by any means—graphic, electronic, or mechanical, including photocopying, recording, or taping or by any information-storage retrieval system—without the written permission of the publisher, except in the case of brief quotations embodied in critical articles and reviews.

Won't Stay Quiet

This memoir is based on experience, memory, notes, and copious amounts of research. Any mistakes are mine and I apologize. Most everyone mentioned has my respect and I appreciate you all for the many lessons.

Published by Eagle Mountain LLC.
Bigfork, Montana USA

Edited by Faydra Romero

Cover and book interior design by Booknook.biz

Printed in the United States of America

For updates and more information, visit Triano.com
Connect with the author at Melissa@Triano.com

ISBN 979-8-218-31697-6 (paperback)
ISBN 979-8-989-67150-2 (hardcover)
ISBN 979-8-218-31698-3 (ebook)

Library Of Congress Cataloging-in-Publication Data is available.

I dedicate this memoir to my son and daughter. The very best part of my life will always be you. My deepest wish is for you to comprehend the times when I was not physically present or emotionally distant, to see the invisible weights that I carried, and that your lives are far less tumultuous than mine. Through these revelations, I hope you garner the strength and wisdom to navigate your own life's challenges and forge a future radiant with understanding, compassion, and resilience. My love for you both is more than words can ever express and will last eternally.

My father, who is the foundation of my existence, both in birth and spirit. I hope this book sheds light on the intricacies of my journey and the reasons behind those "quirky" moments. Thank you, and always know, that my love for you is immeasurable.

To Uncle Gary, our shared moments were cruelly brief, yet their impact is eternal. Your sudden absence left an indelible void, touching all who had the privilege of knowing you. Your legacy, lessons, and memories persist, living vibrantly within us.

Roger, our shared path gifted us our precious children, reflecting the genuine bond we once had. I acknowledge the immense burdens you shouldered, often standing as a lone beacon. While my words may falter, my heart overflows with immense respect and gratitude.

Steve, I honestly don't know what I would have done without you and I know I don't say that enough... maybe not ever. But you have been my anchor for the past 13 years. Your strength, often understated, has been my haven through thick and thin. For every laughter, challenge, and silent moment rich with meaning, I'm eternally thankful. You've been my confidante and rock—my love for you is boundless. I see you.

Acknowledgments

In this journey of *Blossoming Through Adversity*, my heartfelt gratitude extends to Teal Swan, whose spiritual teachings and insights have been a beacon of hope and transformation. Teal, your profound wisdom, and guidance on rethinking the depths of despair and contemplating suicide have been instrumental in not just my survival, but in my flourishing. Your advice did not just reach me; it held me in my darkest hours and illuminated a path forward. You've given me the gift of perspective and the courage to embrace life with renewed vigor. Thank you for your unwavering dedication to helping others find their light in the darkness. Your work didn't just touch my life—it quite literally saved it.

Faydra Romero, my lifelong confidante, I owe you immense gratitude. Not only for taking the first dive into my manuscript but also for lending your keen editing eye and guiding me through the challenging segments of this difficult writing journey. Your unwavering support and friendship have been invaluable. Thank you.

Special thanks are also due to my fellow advocates and everyone at RAINN, whose tireless work and dedication to a sensitive cause have not only inspired me but also provided a platform for voices that, like mine, refused to be silenced. Being a part of the "Won't Stay Quiet" campaign was a turning point in my journey, and I am forever grateful for the opportunity and the support you provide to survivors of violence.

To the countless survivors who have shared their stories with me, your bravery and honesty have been a constant source of inspiration and solidarity. You've reinforced my belief that our shared experiences can forge paths to healing and empowerment.

And to you, the reader, who will take the time to walk this path with me, to hear my story and, perhaps, to see reflections of your own within it—my heartfelt thanks. This story will find its purpose if it helps inspire just one person to keep going, to never give up hope, to learn the art of forgiveness, and to learn to accept the things you can not change and have the courage to change the things you can.

Lastly, I'd like to express my gratitude to the universe for its mysterious ways, for the lessons it's taught me, and for the strength it's given me to transform suffering into growth and silence into storytelling.

A Note from the Author

In fighting for survivors of violence, especially sexual assault, I walk a fine line in a debate often charged with sweeping generalizations. It's a narrative fraught with danger, painting men with broad strokes of villainy and lack of control. Yet, I am a mother to a son I love dearly and a friend to many good men, and I know the reality is not so black and white. Societal norms have historically blurred the lines of consent and respect, sending confusing signals to both genders.

I recall times when society trivialized the seriousness of getting women drunk as a means for men to 'get lucky,' a notion as outdated and wrong as the caveman's club. This was not just misguided; it was harmful, perpetuating a culture that now leaves men in fear of misinterpretation of their actions and intentions.

We must strive for a world where education illuminates the gray areas, where respect is the cornerstone of all interactions, and where the differences between us are celebrated, not weaponized. We must protect and empower all individuals, regardless of gender, to speak and act with integrity.

This delicate balance between advocating for survivors and not alienating half the population is crucial. Men should not be made to live in fear of giving a compliment or offering mentorship. We can promote a culture of consent, mutual respect, and personal responsibility. It's about having open, honest conver-

sations, setting clear boundaries, and fostering an environment where men and women alike can thrive without suspicion or fear.

As a society, we can and must do better—for the survivors whose voices need amplification, for the men and women who stand with us in this fight, and for the future generations who will inherit the world we shape today.

—Melissa Triano

Contents

Acknowledgments vii
A Note from the Author ix
Preface 1
CHAPTER 1: Shadows of a Broken Childhood 5
CHAPTER 2: Seeking Refuge 13
CHAPTER 3: Fractures 19
CHAPTER 4: Resilience in Rebellion 25
CHAPTER 5: The Spotlight's Embrace 31
CHAPTER 6: Neon Dreams and Shifting Sands 37
CHAPTER 7: Amidst the Storm 41
CHAPTER 8: Crossroads and New Horizons 47

    If— (poem by Rudyard Kipling) 52

CHAPTER 9: Unveiling Shadows, Seeking Light 55
CHAPTER 10: Lessons from a Dragon and a Horse 65
CHAPTER 11: Lessons in Humility 69
CHAPTER 12: From Darkness to Dawn 75
CHAPTER 13: Confrontation and Catharsis 85

Chapter 14: Echoes of Deception	91
Chapter 15: A Battle for Justice	97
Chapter 16: Behind the Smile	107
Chapter 17: Sailing Through Stars	115
A Letter to My Son	125
Chapter 18: The Observer and the Observed	131

Informational Chapters

Chapter 19: Lingering Shadows	145
Chapter 20: The Hidden Scars	153
Chapter 21: Recognizing the Unspoken	155
Chapter 22: Silent Whispers	159
Chapter 23: Understanding the Silence in Suffering	163

Note to Survivors of Sexual Assault	167
A Tribute to My Uncle Gary: *In Her Wink: A Mother's Legacy*	169
About the Author	171

Preface

As you embark on this journey through the pages that follow, I invite you to pause for a moment. Breathe. Prepare to dive into a world that, though woven from my personal tapestry of experiences, reflects the broader human condition in its rawest form. This isn't just a story about struggle, trauma, or the complex intricacies of relationships. It's a testament to resilience, a narrative built around the formidable strength of the human spirit, and an intimate confession about the most profound moments that have shaped my existence.

In this book, I unravel parts of my life with an honesty that I once found unfathomable. From the early days marked by youthful innocence, through tumultuous years filled with unexpected encounters, dangerous liaisons, and heart-wrenching betrayals, you'll walk with me through each chapter that has largely defined who I am today. You'll meet a few of the people who've left indelible marks on my soul, for better or for worse, and you'll witness the moments where darkness seemed to swallow me whole.

But most importantly, amidst the shadows, you'll find the light. You'll see the remarkable beauty in healing, the clarity that comes from self-realization, and the profound strength garnered from forgiveness—of others and oneself. You'll discover that even when the path is steeped in fear and trials, there is an innate power within us all: the ability to persevere, to rise, and to redefine our destinies.

This narrative doesn't shy away from the harsh realities of life. It delves into the aftermath of silence and the tumultuous odyssey of speaking one's truth. It's a mirror held up to the societal challenges we face, reflecting the often invisible battles fought within courtroom walls and within the recesses of our minds. It's a candid acknowledgment that our choices, however difficult, carry immense weight.

As a National Speaker for RAINN and a participant in the "Won't Stay Quiet" campaign, I've dedicated myself to advocacy, using my voice to echo the silent whispers of countless survivors.

To those who see echoes of their own stories within these pages, know that you're not alone. To those for whom these experiences are foreign, I ask for your empathy.

For everyone who turns these pages, I hope this book serves as a reminder that we are all fragile beings in one way or another, yet unbreakable in so many more.

And before we delve further into these pages, I ask for your patience and understanding. You see, I am not a seasoned writer with an array of literary tools at my disposal. I am simply a woman whose life has been a testament to survival, a narrative punctuated by trials that some may find difficult to comprehend. As I lay my experiences before you, unvarnished and raw, it is my earnest hope that my story might offer solace to anyone who is struggling to move past their own trauma. Moreover, I wish to kindle a spark of empathy in you, the reader, for the unseen battles that each of us may face. Let us walk this path together with open hearts, supporting one another, for life, with all its beauty, can be an arduous journey.

Welcome to a tiny glimpse of my evolving story!

*"Strength isn't measured by the ability to remain intact,
but by the tenacity to piece together
one's fragments and march forward,
not despite the cracks, but because of them."*

—Melissa Triano

Chapter 1:

Shadows of a Broken Childhood

Healing the Wounds of Yesterday

The world came crashing down in fragments when I was just seven years old, the year my parents decided to end their tumultuous marriage. Life in Tucson, Arizona, was all I knew, a life that oscillated between the blistering heat of the desert sun and the chilling shadows cast by my parents' volatile relationship. My father is a ridiculously handsome and charming man who weathered the brutality he saw in Vietnam. He never spoke about those times to me or anyone. He was always smiling and singing and was my hero. My mother, with her vibrant aura, was the epitome of youthful beauty, sweet and naive fresh out of high school and server at a local hotel restaurant, her laughter a melody that turned heads and, unfortunately, also attracted trouble.

Both stunning in their own right, and free in spirit they were like moths to the flame of each other's radiance. Yet, their beauty was a siren call, luring in admirers who only added fuel to the fire of jealousy and mistrust. Their love story was a fast-paced novel read at a frenetic pace, passionate yet fraught with tension and foreshadowing tragedy. My brother, almost my Irish twin, being just eleven months younger, and I were born into this fervor, innocent but instantly swept up into the vortex of their chaos.

The alcohol didn't help; it was their poison of choice, an accelerant to the flames of discord that danced terrifyingly around our family. It brought out the worst in them, the jealousy, the rage, and the violence that turned our home into a war zone. I still remember the sound of my mother's cry and the sight of my father's raging face, broken glass, and images engraved in my mind like a relentless nightmare.

When the divorce axe finally fell, it split more than just a marriage. My mother, driven by a venomous mix of spite and vengeance, took me with her, severing the bond I had with my father and brother. She painted a veneer of fairness over her decision, claiming it was only right that each parent keep one child. But the truth, which I only came to understand much later, was far more sinister. She wanted to wound my father in the most painful way possible—by ripping me out of his world. I was my father's princess and we were inseparable. In her bid to draw blood, however, it was I who suffered the deepest cut. I was torn from my brother, whom I envied and resented in equal measure, believing he was the lucky one for staying behind with our dad. Little did I know or understand the pain and loss he would endure as well.

The upheaval didn't end there. Seeking the comfort of familiarity and family, my mother dragged me along on her flight back to where she was from, Albuquerque, New Mex-

Chapter 1: Shadows of a Broken Childhood

ico. The physical distance mirrored the growing emotional chasm between my brother and me. My heart ached during the plane rides back and forth, a pendulum swinging between resentment and longing. While my father found his redemption in sobriety, and a new wife displaying a resilience and self-control I deeply admired, my mother tumbled further down the rabbit hole of alcoholism and her addiction to the hollow affirmations she sought from strange men.

The barstools and dim bar lights became my haunt as I was paraded around like a trophy, a child accessory to my mother's tragic performance in dive bars and smoky lounges—largely because she lacked the financial means to hire a sitter. The lowest point of this time period came one Halloween in 1979. Dressed inappropriately as Playboy bunnies, we became a spectacle, my childhood innocence sacrificed at the altar of her need for attention. Confusion warred within me, a child caught in the crossfire of a battle I was never meant to fight.

My mother had no real education and didn't really want to work, so we struggled financially. I remember moving from apartment to apartment and so many cockroaches. Just when I thought our lives had reached rock bottom, Richard Rowand, or "Dick" as he insisted, swaggered and stumbled into our world. My first impression of him was indelibly marked by his showy display of wealth—a $15,000 gold coin necklace, glittering with diamonds. It was a nauseating scene, watching my mother swoon over his extravagance. But that opulent necklace was a noose disguised in gold, pulling us into a cycle of abuse and terror that would haunt my most vulnerable years. I can still smell the gin on his breath.

Dick's presence marked the era of inconceivable terror. His and my mother's love for alcohol, fine dining, and parties was only matched by their capacity for violence. His fists knew no mercy, and my mother's body bore the brunt of his savagery. I was the silent witness, hidden in the shadows, my voice lost in the cacophony of their weekly fights. One night in particular stands out, it was soon after we moved in with him a night when the violence reached a crescendo for the first time. The smell of alcohol was thick in the air, and the sound of my mother's body hitting the wall was a thunderclap in the storm of their relationship. I ran out of my bedroom to see what was happening and I was paralyzed with fear, I huddled under the coffee table, as I watched her slide down the wall to the floor. I watched him rip her pantyhose off of her body and assault her in the most brutal way imaginable. Her eyes met mine, a silent plea echoing in the depths of her gaze. It was a moment of shared helplessness, a tableau of our broken lives.

Morning brought a cruel facade of normalcy. My mother, her body and spirit bruised, carried on as if the horrors of the night before were just a figment of my imagination. I remember asking her if she was okay and if we were going to leave. She drowned the truth in denial, serving up breakfast with a side of lies. This pattern of violence, denial, and isolation became the rhythm of our lives.

Desperate for help, I turned to my grandparents, but my mother's charismatic mask was impenetrable. My stories dismissed as fanciful tales, fell on deaf ears, and I only came across as a bratty kid who simply didn't want her mother married to anyone but my dad. No one believed me. This was pretty hard to imagine, but certainly even harder for an 11-year-old to fabricate. I retreated into a shell, my grades plummeting, my spirit broken. Sleepovers, a rite of passage for other kids, were a distant dream, as the shame

Chapter 1: Shadows of a Broken Childhood

of bed-wetting held me prisoner. I know now that stress caused by traumatic events causes this in children, but no one told me that then, I just carried the shame of nightly bed-wetting. I remember my mother laughing while she would cover my bed with newspapers and make me sleep on them, so I wouldn't ruin the mattress. This lasted until I was at least 13 years old and finally outgrew it.

My fears for my mother's safety rooted me in our home. The looming shadow of Dick's unpredictable temper kept me anchored close, a silent guardian watching from the sidelines. Nights were especially terrifying; the darkness seemed to magnify his volatility. Stepping out meant leaving my mother alone with him, a thought that I couldn't bear for years. So, the world outside was limited, my sphere of safety confined within the walls of our house.

But like a caged bird yearning for escape, I would sometimes reach a breaking point. When the weight of our reality became too much, I'd find refuge at my neighbor's place. Craig, a boy my age, lived there, and our bond was unique. His mother, a regular drinking companion of my own mother's, meant our fates were intertwined from a young age. We were thrust together amidst the chaos of smoky bars, the clinking of glasses, and the unpredictable moods of our inebriated parents. In that unconventional setting, a bond grew between us that felt as deep as that of siblings. We became each other's lifeline, finding solace and understanding in a world that often seemed upside down.

In the gilded cage that Dick constructed, my mother was both a captive and a queen. He lured her with his millions, promising her the world and assuring her she would never need to lift a finger. But behind the opulence lay a dark secret: frequent and heart-wrenching abuse. Every violent episode seemed to be punctuated with extravagant tokens of "apology." Once, it was a shiny new Corvette; another time, he built her an entire restaurant in Taos, New Mexico, named "Taos Ski Valley Junction." This place even boasted an outdoor theater for summer concerts.

Snowmobiles, ski trips, promises of never beating her again, and vows to change became a cyclic pattern, an intoxicating blend of pain and pleasure. But no gift, no trip, and no promise could ever truly compensate for the trauma and torment he inflicted. Abuse, especially when cloaked in luxury and false remorse, is a convoluted web of manipulation. It's imperative to understand that no amount of material luxury can ever justify or erase the scars of abuse. For those ensnared in such a cycle, seeking professional help and counseling is not just an option; it's a lifeline.

Richard Rowand, the man who had dazzled and manipulated so many with his wealth, found himself embroiled in a legal quagmire that unveiled a dark world of cronyism and corruption within the New Mexico legal system. The case, "State v. Ramming," presented a sordid tale of misappropriated state funds designated for disaster projects. In 1984 and 1985 alone, Rowand and his company, CRW Development Corporation, secured $2,800,000 of this money. The projects, however, were riddled with inconsistencies—some weren't genuine disasters, some were marred by excessive change orders, and others showcased subpar or even nonexistent work. The evidence was damning: Dick had defrauded the state out of hundreds of thousands of dollars.

Yet, in a twist that underscored the profound corruption at play, then-Governor Toney Anaya issued an executive order pardoning him for all counts except for one: con-

Chapter 1: Shadows of a Broken Childhood

spiracy. This act was a glaring testament to the deep-seated cronyism that had taken root in the system. But justice has its own way of circling back. That sole charge of conspiracy, which had been left hanging like a Damocles' sword, was eventually dismissed. All charges were dropped, rendering the governor's selective pardon even more questionable in its intent.

However, the legal system wasn't quite done with him. While the initial charges were sidestepped, he later faced accusations of tax evasion. It seemed that while certain arms of the law could be swayed or manipulated, the taxman remained unperturbed and undeterred.

The weight of the legal battles and accusations seemed to amplify the darkness within Dick. With every fresh headline and legal twist, the storm brewing inside him intensified, and tragically, it was my mother who bore the brunt of his tempestuous rage. Towering at 6'4", he was once an athlete, having played football for Rice University. He possessed the stature and strength of a man who had been trained to tackle and dominate on the field.

My mother, in stark contrast, was a petite 5'2", never tipping the scales beyond 120 pounds. She was delicate, almost fragile in her frame, yet she bore an indomitable spirit. But against Rowand's tempests, she often seemed like a delicate flower caught in a hurricane. He treated her with a cruelty that defied understanding, tossing her around as if she weighed nothing.

Each episode of violence left its mark, not just physically but deep within her psyche. It remains a mystery how such a slight figure managed to endure so much pain and so much torment. While her body bore the bruises and scars of his abuse, her spirit and resilience showcased a strength that couldn't be measured in pounds or inches. But every time I think back to those traumatic days, I find myself grappling with a haunting question: How did she, with her tiny frame, withstand such immense cruelty?

My world, once filled with the light of childhood innocence, had become a landscape of shadows. Fear and uncertainty were my constant companions, lurking in every corner of my fractured existence. Though this was the only life I knew, I saw joy and unity in all the other families around me. So, amidst the wreckage, a spark of resolve flickered within me. It was a determination forged in the fires of my ordeal, a silent vow to reclaim the life that was so unjustly stolen from me. But that would not be realized until much later.

Chapter 2:

Seeking Refuge

From Chaos to Calm

By the time the harsh winds of adolescence were upon me, I was weathered beyond my years. High school, a time that should have been filled with the mundane worries of grades and crushes, found me grappling with a weight far heavier than most of my peers could fathom. The chaos that was my constant companion had reached a deafening climax, and I knew something within me had to shift. It was a raw, desperate knowledge: if I didn't change my circumstances, they would end up changing me, and not for the better.

The inaugural year of high school saw me as a member of the dance squad, a "song leader." Our role transcended mere rhythmical movements; we were there to rally spirits, to infuse vigor into the crowd that rooted for our football heroes under the Friday night lights. Amongst these heroes was Todd, the star quarterback, the heartthrob who was one of my closest friend's boyfriends and he became my friend too. Our trio was inseparable, sharing laughter and dreams during the after-school hours and around the mesmerizing flames of bonfire parties.

I remember one time, my mom and Dick decided to go to Taos to visit the restaurant, but this time they would go alone. The thrill of an empty house is too tempting for any teenager. With my parents gone for the weekend, the allure of rebellion was too much to resist. Cameron, Todd's guitar-playing heartthrob friend who had captured my and seemingly every other girl's attention, was my ticket to popularity. What started as an invitation to him alone quickly escalated, and soon enough, the house was swarming with hundreds of kids from school. It wasn't just a party; it was an epic house takeover.

Among the chaos, there were games of "quarters" (a game where you bounce a quarter off the table and if you make it in the shot glass the other person drinks and if you miss you drink) that marred my mother's pristine table with countless divots. So much so that by the end of the night the table looked like it was made that way. Each dent was a testament to the wildness of the night. The kitchen turned into a battleground for a whip-cream fight, leaving behind a lingering sour smell that hinted at the disaster that had unfolded. Staircase walls, smeared with denim stains, bore witness to countless kids' playful descents. By morning, the house was a warzone, its once immaculate spaces now scarred by youthful recklessness.

Panicking at the thought of my mother's reaction to the destruction, I made a rash decision for a 13-year-old: I took her Corvette, a symbol of her luxury and pride, to the store to purchase cleaning supplies. No one had ever taught me to drive. I taught myself. But fate had another twist in store. They returned home earlier than expected,

Chapter 2: Seeking Refuge

worried about their decision to leave me unattended. As I approached the driveway, the familiar sound of the garage door opening signaled a moment of pure dread. My mother's legs came into view, and in my panic, I forgot everything about driving. Slamming both feet down on the pedals in a desperate attempt to stop, the powerful Corvette lunged forward instead. My heart raced as my mother lept out of the path of the speeding car, which crashed into our freezer, pushing it into the house through the back wall. When I shifted to reverse, the dislodged freezer door collapsed onto the windshield of the Corvette.

My mind raced, adrenaline coursing through my veins. Without a second thought, I bolted from the car and ran, leaving behind the chaos of a weekend I'd never forget.

My mind was consumed by fear after the debacle at home. In every possible scenario I played out, I imagined Dick's towering figure, his anger unleashing itself on me with a force I had witnessed too many times on my mother. For a child who always tried to walk the straight path, always so conscious of every step, this was an aberration. It was an act of pure, unbridled rebellion, and I was certain the punishment would be equally severe.

When they finally tracked me down at a friend's house a couple of days later, I braced myself for the storm. But, to my astonishment, there was no anger, no shout, no threat. Instead, they laughed. It wasn't just a small chuckle; it was genuine, hearty laughter. The kind that comes from deep within, surprising even those expressing it.

The weight that had been pressing down on me lifted instantaneously. In that moment, amidst the laughter and relief, I realized that sometimes, even the gravest mistakes can be met with understanding and compassion. Their reaction was a testament to the unpredictability of life and people, reminding me that even in our darkest moments, there's always a chance for light.

It dawned on me, amidst the unpredictability of their reactions, that perhaps the barometer for their anger was skewed. The years of trauma, the chaos, and the storms that I had been subjected to had perhaps numbed them to the regular nuances of parenthood. Their indifference to my mistakes, which might have been a sigh of relief for any other child, only served as a stark reminder of our fractured relationship.

Every time they shrugged off my actions, it echoed a deeper sentiment: their seeming detachment from my well-being. The laughter that day wasn't just them finding humor in a teenager's misadventure; it was a reflection of their inability to genuinely connect, to understand the depth of emotions and fears that had driven me to act out in the first place.

While some might envy a life free from consequences, for me, their indifference was more cutting than any punishment. It was a stark reminder that amidst the turbulence of our household, perhaps what I yearned for most was not the freedom from retribution, but the simple acknowledgment of my existence and feelings.

One unsuspecting day, later that same year, Todd showed up at my house, alone. I remember he knocked on my door and when I answered he asked if my mother was home. I told him she was at the store and he immediately grabbed me, before I knew it, I was on the ground and he was forcing himself on me. He tore my shirt off and my screams, if there were any, were lost in the vortex of his aggression and my disbelief.

Chapter 2: Seeking Refuge

Salvation arrived in the form of my mother, her entrance through the garage door a divine intervention. Yet, her stillness, her paralysis as she witnessed the tail end of my ordeal, sowed seeds of confusion and betrayal., She watched motionless as he jumped up and ran out the front door.

The aftermath unfolded on our living room couch, a scene of superficial comfort. Her words, intended as solace, fell like leaden shrapnel, embedding themselves within me. "You are fine," She said. "That's just how boys are around beautiful girls, they can't control themselves!" I remember her laughing.

The dismissal of the atrocity as a mere consequence of male impulse and my supposed allure was a secondary violation, one that demanded silence and complicity. But, with a mix of trepidation and a yearning so intense it almost hurt, I made a choice. Right then and there—a choice that was both an ending and a beginning. I decided to leave the turmoil of my mother's home, to escape the storm and seek out the solace that had eluded me for so long. My destination? Tucson, the city that held the fragmented memories of childhood before it was shattered, where my father, brother, stepmother, cousins, and aunts and uncles resided. In my heart, it was a pilgrimage, a journey back to a place where I hoped to find not just safety, but the peace that had been such a foreign concept, an elusive shadow, for as long as I could remember.

The day I left Albuquerque was one painted with the hues of bittersweet freedom. The sight of my mother, a figure as tragically beautiful as she was broken, faded into the horizon as the miles between us stretched wider. There was guilt, yes, and a hollow pit of sadness—emotions that would take years to fully unpack—but overriding it all was a sense of determination, a silent mantra repeating in my mind that I was doing this to save myself. And a knowing that I could never save her. Nor was it my place to even try.

Arriving in Tucson was like drawing a breath after years of suffocation. Here, amidst the familiar desert landscape, with its sun-bleached sands and towering cacti standing sentinel against the azure sky, I dared to hope. My father, with his quiet strength and the sobriety that was his hard-won battle scar, welcomed me with open arms. Beside him stood my stepmother, a beacon of kindness and stability I hadn't realized I'd been so desperate for, nor could I fully come to accept until much later in life. We struggled with finding our place in each other's lives. I suppose then I resented her too for building a life with my father that my own mother could never accomplish.

Even as I settled into this new haven, the specters of my past were not so easily left behind. They lurked in the nightmares that disturbed my sleep and in the reflexive flinch that came with sudden movements and loud voices. Healing, I came to understand, wasn't a switch to be flipped, but a journey to be undertaken, step by painstaking step.

High school there unfolded with its own set of challenges, but now, there was a foundation of support beneath me that hadn't been there before. I wasn't alone in my battles, and that knowledge was like a balm to my scarred psyche. There were days of light and laughter with my beloved brother, cousins, and friends, moments where I caught glimpses of the carefree teenager I could've been had circumstances been different. And while the shadows of my past never fully receded for we carry our histories within us wherever we go—they no longer held the power they once did. Or did they?

CHAPTER 3:

Fractures

The Fragility and Fortitude of Life

In the solace of my father's home, I believed I had found refuge. Yet, life, in its relentless unpredictability, wasn't done throwing storms my way. As we navigated the nuances of a rekindled relationship, a new tempest was brewing: my grandfather, the patriarch whose quiet strength had been a subtle constant in my life, was waging a war against cancer. The disease, merciless and unyielding, was a battle he couldn't win. Watching him slowly wither away is one of the most devastating memories I recall.

Like me, the bond between my father and his own was not just one of blood, but one of profound admiration and deepest affinity. My father didn't just see his dad as a parent but as the epitome of his world, an idol in flesh and blood, whose very presence was a guiding star in the dark sky of life. Their connection was further enriched and complicated by the strands of their professional lives, interwoven in the daily grind, as they worked shoulder to shoulder. This wasn't just familial love; it was a comradeship, the kind that is etched in every laugh shared over a lunch break, every bead of sweat shed in unison, every shared glance acknowledging that the other understands you, fundamentally and completely.

So, when the formidable figure we affectionately called "Pop" was besieged by the unforgiving claws of lung cancer, it wasn't just a disease claiming its due. It was as if the very foundation of my father's universe was crumbling. The diagnosis hit him like a wayward bullet, unexpected despite all the signs, and it tore through the fortified walls he had built around his emotions. My father, a rock through tempests before this, was suddenly rendered vulnerable, his pain an exposed nerve, raw and unyielding. He moved through those last months with Pop more like a shadow than a man, the weight of impending loss anchoring him to a reality he yearned to escape my father during this time was like witnessing the slow fracturing of a rock long thought unbreakable. He was splintering under the weight of impending loss, and the cracks were beginning to show. His pain was a silent, palpable entity in our home, a relentless reminder of the fragility of our human lives. When my grandfather finally succumbed to his illness, what followed was not just an outpouring of grief but a landslide of complications that none of us had foreseen.

Inheriting my grandfather's business should have been a saving grace, a legacy passed from one generation to the next. Instead, it was a Trojan horse, a gift that carried within it a hidden onslaught. Debt, like a stealthy thief, crept into our lives, and with it, a myriad of tensions that strained the already fragile threads holding our family together.

But the true earthquake came on an ordinary day, its ordinariness a stark contrast to the upheaval it would bring. Playing truant from school, a small act of rebellion, I stum-

Chapter 3: Fractures

bled upon a truth that would shatter the precarious peace I'd found: my father, my hero, the man who'd resurrected from his own demons to provide me with a haven, was entangled in an affair. I ditched school that day and was driving across town. There at a traffic light, I saw my dad's car, but he wasn't alone. I ducked, terrified he would catch me not where I should have been, but he was too captivated to notice me with the blonde woman in his passenger seat. The image seared itself into my mind—him and her, locked in a passionate kiss that betrayed everything I thought I knew.

In that moment, my world fractured. The trust that I'd painstakingly rebuilt, not just in my father but in the idea that maybe, just maybe, there was some good in this world, crumbled. I was adrift, the debris of my shattered beliefs threatening to pull me under.

I never told him or anyone else that I saw them. I didn't know what to do with that information and I avoided confrontation back then at all costs.

Reflecting back, my behavior towards my stepmother in those tumultuous teenage years now tinges my memories with regret. There was a storm of emotions, confusion, and rebellion melding within me, manifesting in sharp words and curt responses whenever she reached out. Every attempt of hers to breach the walls I'd recklessly erected was met with the coldness of a winter squall, my youthful ignorance convincing me that I was warding off unwanted intrusion. But she was not the enemy I painted her to be in the vibrant, misguided colors of adolescence.

My stepmother weathered my rudeness, an unwavering pillar against the gale of my angst. Her patience was a silent lesson, her persistence a quiet reminder that family isn't about perfection, but about endurance; it's about standing firm in the face of hurricanes, knowing well that the skies will clear. It took the wisdom that comes with fading youth and the softening lens of time to see that what I had perceived as interference was, in fact, a hand extended in solidarity, an offer of kinship in a world that can, at times, be unkind. My rudeness, a barrier then, now stands as a testament to her resilience and capacity for understanding, love, and forgiveness.

Soon after, a letter from my mother arrived, carrying more than just her words. Tucked inside was a newspaper clipping, its headline screaming a truth that caused my world to crumble: Todd, once celebrated as Albuquerque's star quarterback, was now a convicted monster, guilty of eleven counts of rape. Numbness enveloped me as I retreated to the solitude of my room, the haunting melody of Bette Midler's "The Rose" becoming the soundtrack to my sorrow, playing on an endless loop that mirrored the ceaseless cycle of my thoughts.

There, amidst the music's melancholic embrace, tears found me. They streamed down, hot and unbidden, not just for my own suppressed pain, but for the other girls, the ones I believed I'd failed. The weight of unspoken truth bore down on me, a pang of crushing guilt whispering that my silence had been their cage.

Why had my mother sent that article? Her accompanying note bore no mention of it, no words of solace, just a stark, cutting reminder of the boy Todd truly was—a silent scream inked in black and white. It felt like a gash in my already wounded spirit, a confirmation of the darkness lurking in human guise.

At that moment, something within me fractured. Trust became a concept too brittle to hold, hope a cruel illusion.

Chapter 3: Fractures

I felt like a spectral figure, drifting on the fringes of a world I no longer recognized, where malice moved unhindered and innocence lay trampled. What kind of world is this? The thought tormented me. A world I no longer wanted any stake in.

At just 16, I'd witnessed depths of depravity that eclipsed any youthful illusions. And I knew, with a certainty that anchored in my soul, I could never be the same again.

And so, I made a choice—a quiet, desperate decision, born from a place of unimaginable pain. I had no trust in anyone or anything. I decided to end the turmoil once and for all. Home alone, the house's silence a stark reminder of my isolation, I downed a bottle of Xanax pills I found in my father's bathroom, one after the other, a lethal chain meant to link me to a peace I believed I could only find in oblivion.

But fate, it seemed, wasn't done with me yet. A high school friend, Teresa, an unsuspecting guardian angel, one who had also found herself in the depths of depression at one point in her life, dialed my number that day. Between the fog of pills and despair, I answered, my voice a lifeline I didn't even know I was throwing. Alarm translated into action, and soon, the wail of sirens pierced the heavy silence, the paramedics a flurry of urgency against the slow lull of my fading consciousness.

I woke to the harsh lights of a hospital room, the beeping of machines a jarring symphony that anchored me back to the reality I'd tried to flee.

It was the first time I had ever actually seen my dad cry and it destroyed me to see him so scared. There, in the aftermath of my shattered resolve, I understood: that my journey was far from over. Healing wasn't just in the absence of pain but in the acceptance of it, in the acknowledgment that life, with its fractures and fissures, might still be worth enduring.

Survival, I soon realized, wasn't a choice but a mandate, an undeniable call to endure, to face the storms yet to come.

The song, The Rose, explores the nature of love, comparing it to a flower that might seem fragile but has roots deeply set in the earth. It emphasizes that, despite the pain and fear often associated with love, the feeling is as enduring and natural as a rose that grows from the ground. The song suggests that love's true essence is found in the soul, and even if one faces heartbreak, love's essence remains, waiting to bloom again.

CHAPTER 4:

Resilience in Rebellion

As the sweltering Arizona summer arrived before my senior year, life presented its challenges in rapid, unrelenting succession. However, the curveball that completely blindsided me was my parent's decision to leave Arizona, a desperate attempt to mend their marriage and get away from the jaded memories. They expected blind compliance, assuming my brother and I would uproot our lives to follow them into this uncertainty. My brother was happy to go with them, but years of constant turmoil that I had known, had ignited a fierce defiance within me. I refused to be a passive participant in my own life, dragged along by the decisions of others. My connections—friends, cousins, my aunt, and uncle—they were now the constants in a life marred by instability. Leaving them was out of the question.

For the first time, I asserted my independence, choosing to stay at just 17 years old. They begrudgingly offered a compromise—an apartment owned by my uncle. My best friend's mother Denise swore to keep an eye on us and that she would allow her to also live there with me. It was a grungy place in a terrible location, but it was a promise of stability. Yet, life wasn't done challenging me. They left me with two cars and no money, casually suggesting I sell the cars—an impossibility since they weren't in my name. Their refusal to help when I reached out, dangling on the precipice of despair, steeled my resolve. I would later learn that they simply could not help. At that point, they were struggling financially and were doing everything they could to survive themselves.

Fueled by hunger and righteous anger, I took matters into my own hands. I painstakingly dismantled those cars, selling them piece by piece. Each transaction was a victory, a step toward self-reliance. It was a silent rebellion, an assertion of control in a life that felt perpetually chaotic.

In the year 1987, as the world around me buzzed with the hope and promise that the close of a decade often brings, I found myself caught in a web of challenges. I grappled not only with the throbbing absence of my parents but also with the tangible echoes of their presence: two vehicles, each holding its own trove of memories and lessons.

The Lincoln was a marvel in its own right. It bore the kind of regal presence that only a Lincoln can, complete with an in-car phone. In a time when mobile communication was a burgeoning luxury, this car phone stood as a testament to the affluence of days gone by. But beneath its polished exterior and upscale features, it held a secret: a dire need for an oil change. Ignorance and youth made for a disastrous combination, leading to the day it threw a rod. Its once robust engine fell silent, rendering it a metallic behemoth, brimming with memories but void of motion. With the car title not in my possession and the Lincoln otherwise totaled, my hands were tied. The only path forward was to painstakingly part it out, selling each component to those who saw value in them. Every transaction was bittersweet, a letting go of memories intertwined with the steel and leather of that majestic vehicle.

Each time I glanced at its "40 more" license plate, I pondered its significance. Was it a playful nod to my father's 40th birthday, or had it transformed into a marker of endurance, hinting at the challenges yet to come? Parallel to the tale of the Lincoln was the narrative of the 1965 Ford Mustang. Pristine white with a light green interior that harkened back to a different era, it boasted an 8-track cassette player and was completely original.

As these cars slowly but surely found new homes, piece by piece, my own life was a constant exercise in frugality. Every penny counted. Days were punctuated with meals that spoke of simplicity and survival: the salted broth of ramen noodles, the creamy texture of macaroni and cheese, and the crisp, salty bite of fried bologna sandwiches. They were humble meals, yet they carried the weight of my determination and tenacity.

Life also took me to the doors of Kentucky Fried Chicken, courtesy of a friend's father who owned the KFC outlets in Tucson. They hired me to work there and while the experience left me drenched in grease and yearning for a break, it also instilled in me the values of hard work and persistence.

The journey, marked by bus rides, grease stains, and the echoes of two cars, was arduous. Yet, it wasn't without its silver linings. Each challenge faced, each memory released into the world, and every coin saved added layers to my resilience. They were the foundational stones upon which my future was to be built, a testament to a young soul's ability to blossom through adversity.

At the very immature age of 18, independence wasn't just a choice for me—it was my entire reality. While my peers were navigating the quintessential dramas of high school, I was braving the world alone, juggling the myriad challenges that come with living on my own. The traditional path of education slipped from my grasp; by the middle of what should have been a pivotal year, I had officially left high school. Now labeled a quitter by my family, but can you really quit something that quit you first? No, you leave.

High school, with its cacophony of adolescent chaos, branded me with another label I wasn't entirely aware of. Whispers, like tendrils of smoke, wound their way through hallways and classrooms, crafting a narrative of my sexuality before I'd even had the chance to understand it myself. They called me a lesbian because I rejected every boy who tried to date me. A dike, words they wielded like weapons, though their true weight wouldn't land on my shoulders until years later. Back then, I only understood that I was an anomaly—a square peg amidst the round holes of teenage norms.

While my friends were dizzy with the newfound rush of boys and the dizzying maze of teenage desire, I stood on the sidelines, an island in the turbulent sea of adolescent romance. Boys, to my untutored mind, were an alien species, repulsive in a way I couldn't articulate. My perception of intimacy had been unwittingly, and irrevocably, skewed not only by my mother's absurd situation but by a childhood glimpse of our dogs locked in a primal embrace. That image festered in the shadows of ignorance, thanks to the glaring absence of comprehensive sex education, morphing the male anatomy in my imagination into something grotesque and canine-like.

Chapter 4: Resilience in Rebellion

So, I recoiled from my friends' tales of their trysts, my disgust rooted not in judgment but in the ghastly visuals that plagued my mind. In a world teetering on the brink of adulthood, my misconception was an unlikely armor, one that, in a twist of fate, safeguarded me from the all-too-common tale of teenage pregnancy.

The truth of my revulsion remained a secret until one day, in the sanctuary of my room, my best friend Shantel, amidst yet another story, paused to confront the elephant in the room. Her question, laced with genuine confusion, finally pried the truth from my lips.

And as the absurdity of my confession hung in the air, it was met with the kind of unrestrained laughter that only true friendship allows. Shantel toppled off the bed, her laughter a melody that rang through the room, a moment of pure, unadulterated hilarity. Looking back now, it's a cherished memory, a snapshot of innocence, ignorance, and the beautiful folly of youth.

The labels began long before that, though. "Disruptive," they called me, an instigator who posed too many questions and never followed the beaten path. My inquisitiveness was met with annoyance rather than encouragement. Educators, unequipped to handle my relentless curiosity, pigeonholed me as a candidate for special education. They painted me as impaired, asserting a learning disability where there was none. This misconception wasn't just erroneous; it was a disservice to my intellectual potential and a heavy hit to my self-esteem.

Back then, I admit, school wasn't my priority. Yet, my disinterest was misconstrued as incapacity. Years later, an IQ test would reveal a score of 146, highlighting a stark contrast between perception and reality. My mind was a whirlwind of questions, many of which left my teachers dumbfounded. I wasn't being difficult; I was eager for knowledge beyond the standard curriculum, a fact more evident now given my undying passion for learning and expanding my horizons.

However, during those formative years, patience was a virtue I hadn't yet acquired. In fact, it's a virtue I still work on to this day. The trauma that percolated every aspect of my young life didn't afford me the luxury of mental spaciousness necessary to articulate my thoughts. My educational journey was marred by instability—3 different elementary schools, 3 different middle schools, and 4 distinct high schools. I didn't just adapt to change; I became its master.

This constant state of flux, however, took its toll. Each move, each adjustment was a jarring reminder of life's unpredictability. My resilience was both a shield and a sword—protecting me, driving me—but also, in quiet moments, a weight heavy with solitude. Yet, it's this very resilience and inherent rebellion against preconceived notions that fueled my journey of self-discovery and learning.

The narrative of my educational experience isn't one of failure but of a profound mismatch between a rigid system and a free-spirited learner. It's a testament to the resilience of a young individual thriving in the face of adversity and the rebellion against a one-size-fits-all approach to education. And above all, it's an ongoing journey of learning, unlearning, and relearning, a passion undimmed by the trials of my past.

That year, and the ones that followed, resilience took on a new meaning. It was more than survival; it was reveling in life's tempest, finding joy amidst adversity. I was no longer defined by my circumstances but by my resilience.

CHAPTER 5:

The Spotlight's Embrace

Mercedes Rises

Arizona nights were never really dark; the neon signs saw to that. They were a beacon, and for me, they marked the beginning of something... unconventional. It all started with a newspaper—the kind with coffee stains and stories of people you'd never meet. My best friend waved it in front of me like a flag of surrender, but it felt more like a challenge. There, amid the black and white, was Ginger—not a spice, but a stripper. She was making a fortune, the paper said, in just one night at the show club. More money than we could make in a month, doing boring jobs that ate away at our souls.

I'd always been a fantastic dancer. Not yet in clubs, but in school, in my living room, under the streetlights, anywhere the music reached. My body knew rhythms no one else heard. But it wasn't just my moves that drew eyes; it was my curves, too. My abnormally large breasts had been the subject of much teasing, of unwanted attention, of shame. But Ginger's story, her power, it made me think.

Maybe the things I'd been ashamed of could be my greatest assets. Also, I think I wanted to make my father angry. Actually, I know I did. One of the businesses that my father had inherited when my grandfather passed was a strip club and that is where he met the blonde in his car, so there was a small part of me that wanted desperately for a glimpse inside that sinful world.

The neon lights were dazzling, reflecting off sequins and satin as I, a mere 19-year-old, stood hesitantly at the entrance of the town's most renowned exotic show club. It was my birthday, a day of crossing thresholds, and here was an unexpected one. Inside, elegance and sensuality danced together, women moving with a confidence so palpable, it was almost a separate entity in the room. They were goddesses in gowns, commanding the stage in ways I'd only caught glimpses of in the risqué corners of late-night movies.

I was no goddess. Shyness was my cloak, and insecurity, my constant companion, whispering critiques about my body—a body that dared to defy the norms of 1989, where the whispers of the silicone revolution were only just beginning. My natural curves set me apart in a way that attracted mockery instead of admiration during those cruel middle school and high school years. I felt like an imposter in a realm I couldn't possibly belong to.

Overwhelmed, I ran out of the club and fled. But fate, in the guise of the club manager Jean, wasn't having it. He saw something in me—a potential I hadn't dared to acknowledge. With a persuasive assurance, he ushered me back into a world I was poised to abandon, back to the dressing room sanctum where goddesses prepped for their adoration. They were having an amateur contest there that night and they enticed me to enter.

Chapter 5: The Spotlight's Embrace

They rallied around me, these women, with camaraderie unexpected in a space I assumed was reserved for rivalry. A slinky outfit was selected, a persona crafted. They asked for a name, and from the whirlwind of my mind emerged "Mercedes," plucked from the reels of a favorite 1988 film, "License to Drive". And of course, they gave me a shot of tequila, liquid courage they said.

Stepping onto the pitch-black stage, the opening synths of a mix the DJ crafted of "Riding the Storm Out", by REO Speedwagon and "Relax" by Frankie Goes to Hollywood enveloped me. The room was awash with smoke and frenzied lighting, but I closed it all out. The world narrowed to just me and the music. I was alone, and for the first time, that solitude was empowering rather than isolating. My body, the subject of so much scorn, became an instrument of artistry and allure. I danced. I became Mercedes.

And they rose. Each and every patron in a standing ovation, a scene unheard of in the annals of strip club lore. Their applause was a baptism, washing away the years of doubt and derision, revealing someone I had never known myself to be. I descended from the stage not just victorious in the contest, but reborn. In my arms, I carried the weight of thousands of dollars, but in my spirit, I carried something priceless: the discovery of my own power.

Back in the dressing room, amid a chorus of cheers, all the girls were astounded—not a single bra strap had slipped, yet the crowd had been impressively generous. They pointed, half in jest, half in admiration, to the untouched state of my top, as if to say the art of allure lies not in what you bare, but in what you dare to keep covered. I was hooked—not just on the thrill of performance, but on the intoxicating drug of self-confidence. From that night, Mercedes didn't just live on the stage; she walked with me, showing me that within my own skin, there was a goddess who had been waiting to rise. So, I embraced defiance once more. The show club's lights were blinding, but the darkness was where I found myself. The stage became my domain, the pole my partner, and the music my guide. When I danced, everything else faded away—the bills, the past, the judgments. There was only the music, my movements, and the rain of money that followed. I was another person in a fantasy world who had no fear.

It's funny, isn't it? I'd spent so long hating my breasts, my body. I thought they made me look fat in clothes. But up there, in the neon glow, they were my armor, my strength. I was no longer the girl with the "gigantic breasts" to be teased. I was the woman who wielded her femininity like a weapon, who drew eyes and wallets without a single touch. I was powerful. I was in control.

It wasn't about the men or what they wanted. It was about taking something I'd been taught to be ashamed of and turning it into my greatest strength. It was about survival, sure. But it was also about defiance, about claiming something uniquely mine and using it to forge my path.

They called me by a different name, those faceless crowds, but they never really saw me. They saw the persona, the fantasy. And beneath the makeup and the allure, there was a girl who had taken every curveball life had thrown and swung right back. A girl writing her own story, one hundred dollar bill at a time.

In this momentary chapter of my life as an exotic dancer, I crossed paths with individuals from worlds both dazzling and dangerous. The allure of fame brushed shoulders with the shadows of infamy as I mingled with celebrities and

Chapter 5: The Spotlight's Embrace

danced on the fringes of darkness where drug lords and cartels—Mexican, Colombian, and Italian—brokered power in hushed tones. These were my formative years, a time of rapid awakening and harsh lessons, a paradoxical haven that, despite my retrospective shame, emerged as an unlikely salvation.

In presenting this chapter of my life, I tread carefully on the shimmering reflections of memories, acutely aware of the dual edges that this time holds. It's crucial to understand that my recounting of experiences within the pulsating walls of exotic nightclubs is by no means an endorsement or an invitation to glorify this world. The neon lights and rhythmic beats, the allure of what seemed like unrestrained freedom and empowerment—these are but fragments of a much larger, more complex picture.

The landscape of these clubs, as I perceive them now, has undergone tectonic shifts. Time, regulations, and societal changes have reshaped their foundations in ways I couldn't have foreseen in the midst of my own journey. There's a gritty reality beneath the glitz, a shadow that trails behind the spotlight, often unseen or deliberately ignored. It's a world that harbors as much desperation and danger as it does dreams and daring.

I unravel these memories with a sense of responsibility, acknowledging that the path I walked was fraught with unseen precipices and silent battles. There were moments shrouded in darkness, instances where dignity was a luxury and safety was a gift. This chapter, while it may glisten with tales of triumph and echoes of laughter, also bears the indelible scars of experiences that were anything but glorious.

So, as I entrust you with this fragment of my past, I urge you to read between the lines, to see beyond the allure and recognize the human vulnerabilities that were, and perhaps still are, an intrinsic part of this world. It's a tapestry of resilience, but also a testament to the complexities of a life less ordinary, and a silent reminder that not all that glitters is gold.

Within the pulsing lights and veiled corners of that world, I was privy to the rawest exhibitions of human nature. The experience was an education unlike any other, teaching me the complex tapestry of humanity—its contradictions, its hidden kindnesses, its unexpected cruelties. It was there I learned that appearances often betray the truth; those cloaked in respectability weren't always noble, and amongst those society had branded as outcasts, I discovered unexpected reservoirs of kindness and honor. This journey peeled back the layers of my preconceptions, revealing the startling truth about our shared humanity: we are a spectrum, each of us capable of light and darkness, and often, it's in the most unexpected places that we witness the purest reflections of our collective soul.

CHAPTER 6:

Neon Dreams and Shifting Sands

A Dance of Destiny and Defiance

In the dimly lit enclave of the club, where neon dreams danced across the walls, my life took an unexpected turn. The owners, Tim and Dana, saw potential in my eyes—a fire not extinguished by the heady nightclub air. Their proposition was simple, yet transformative: work the nights away, pursue college by day, and they would match every dollar I earned, investing in my education as I invested in their establishment. It was there, amidst whispers and desires, that I stepped out of the long shadows, using the club's sultry stigma as a springboard for my aspirations.

Traveling became a part of my routine, a circuit of shows that filled my pockets and broadened my world. The faces of the famous blurred into the crowds, their stories interwoven with mine as I graced their parties, a silent student of their public plays and hidden follies. Music became my muse, guiding me from an insecure past to a present pulsating with confidence and purpose.

The '90s swirled around us like a desert storm, bringing together lives as disparate as they were vibrant. Among them were my Uncle Gary, a Tucson visionary with his roots deep in arid soil, and his wife Pamela, a magnetic force in her own right. Their orbit collided with Donald Trump and Marla Maples, icons of the age, atop a New York helipad—a confluence of destinies that no one could have predicted.

Their camaraderie blossomed from the heights of Manhattan to the heart of Tucson, where even the larger-than-life Trump found commonality in the rugged beauty of Arizona, cheering alongside fans with my uncle at a U of A Wildcats game. It was at a dinner, abuzz with laughter and energetic discussions, where I dared to touch upon a divisive topic. This move drew a gentle reprimand from my uncle, who was cautious about the dinner's conversational norms. Yet Donald, with a spark of humor in his eyes, welcomed my bold inquisitiveness, recognizing the wisdom and fearlessness that belied my youth.

These moments are more than memories; they are the lessons of kinship and respect, learned from mentors in unexpected guises. My esteem for Donald stemmed from his unexpected humor, his kinship with my uncle, and his acknowledgment of a spirited debate. He told me to always speak my mind and that there wasn't a question I should ever be afraid to ask or have a point that I didn't dare make. It's a tribute to those unafraid to speak their minds, who relentlessly pursue the truth and discover kindred spirits in extraordinary places.

Yet, as college beckoned, my nocturnal endeavors soon came to light under Uncle Gary's scrutiny. He implored

Chapter 6: Neon Dreams and Shifting Sands

me to abandon the neon glow for a more traditional career path, for the sake of our family's name. But I wasn't ready to relinquish my hard-won independence or the electric thrill of the nightlife. I promised to consider his offer, knowing my dance was far from over.

Soon after and seemingly orchestrated by destiny, Rich entered my life. A California boy with a crooked smile that echoed the charm of a young Elvis. Our connection was instantaneous, a love story penned in the stars. We fell in love instantly and before long, planned our future together.

Our first Christmas was in Menlo Park, California, where his parents gifted us a tropical getaway for spring break to the garden island of Kauai, Hawaii. I had never seen anything so amazing in my life. I felt like I was in the King Kong movie and never wanted to leave. So once we got back to Tucson, we finished that semester of school sold everything we owned, and bought two one-way tickets back to Kauai. His parents, were not very happy with me then, but we promised we would resume school in a year or two, so they agreed to our break.

We sold our cars for the money and took a limo from Tucson to the Phoenix airport. Once we checked our bags and made it to the gate, he got down on one knee and proposed to me! It was a whirlwind chapter, brimming with the kind of heartfelt romance and serendipitous encounters that could easily spark the plot of a rom-com. Of course I said, YES! However, I insisted we have a long engagement. While we had a lot of fun together, I wasn't completely sold on the idea of a forever commitment with him.

Kauai welcomed us, a couple intoxicated by life, love, and the freedom of youth. We lived for the surf, the sun, and the sheer joy of each new day. But with time, the island's allure faded; the nightlife's siren call grew faint, and the doubts began to creep in. Trust, which was a delicate dance for me, became even more precarious amid the era's health crisis. The specter of AIDS loomed large, an ominous backdrop to our island idyll.

In 1992, trust was a gamble, with stakes raised by the ever-present threat of a global epidemic. My guarded heart, shaped by a childhood filled with unsafe relationships, wrestled with the vulnerability of commitment. Entrusting someone, especially someone as untamed as my fiancé, with both my emotional and physical safety felt like a monumental gamble.

Rich was a vision, the kind that caught every eye and turned each head. Both women and men seemed magnetically drawn to him, their advances were as blatant as they were persistent. At the young age of 22, I fully subscribed to the notion that a man's fidelity was only a measure of his opportunities, leaving me in a perpetual state of vigilance, bracing for the inevitable moment when our perfect world would come undone.

As if on cue from the unpredictable script of existence, life served a stark reminder that control was but an illusion. A Category 5 hurricane, vast and relentless, set a course for our island sanctuary, threatening to unravel the façade of our idyllic retreat and test the foundations of everything we had built.

CHAPTER 7:

Amidst the Storm

Iniki 9/11/1992

911 is the number you call when there is an emergency. I'll never forget it. The date it came was September 11, 1992, a day etched into the minds of those on Kauai, not for global events, but for a cataclysm of nature that would challenge the very spirit of the entire island. It was a force of unbridled ferocity, that made landfall. Its winds, like furious sentinels, reached 150 miles per hour, with wrathful gusts that soared even higher, reshaping reality as we knew it.

The news assured us that the brunt of the storm would hit Oahu and still Rich insisted we would be safe in our house and that we did not need to leave. However, the neighbors and local Hawaiians told me confidently that the storm was coming for us. How do you know, I asked? They explained, "Look at the sky, there is no breeze and there are no insects. None at all. This is how we know." And they certainly proved to be right. They knew from living long enough on these islands the signs that no weatherman could ever predict.

The following day the storm changed course. Now a direct path toward our garden island.

Before Iniki, hurricanes were abstract, events that plagued other places. But as the skies darkened and the air bristled with electricity, abstraction became a terrifying reality. We battened down the hatches, so to speak, yet nothing could have prepared us for the onslaught. Roofs, once the sanctity of shelter, became airborne debris. Trees, those ancient island guardians, were uprooted and turned into nature's own missiles. Sounds, not of rain or wind, but of destruction, filled the air. It was as if the storm was alive, a growling beast of mythical proportion.

In the eye of the storm, we hid in the bathroom, our bodies pressed into each other, the only sanctuary against the chaos outside. We weren't just huddled; we were entwined, clinging to a shred of normalcy as our makeshift shield—a mattress—barricaded us against nature's wrath. We had a radio with us, its familiar hum of a comforting thread against the growing storm , but it didn't. We clung to every crackled report, every update a beacon in the tempest that raged around us. But nature, in its raw and untamed splendor eventually claimed even that solace, its fury reaching a crescendo that silenced the radio tower, leaving us with nothing but the storm's howling refrain. Outside, Iniki was a wild beast, its howls like those of an ancient witch cursing the land. With every shingle ripped away by the tempest, it felt as though fragments of our hope were being torn from us, leaving us naked to the fury. The room flickered with an eerie brightness as rain invaded our refuge, baptizing us in sheer terror. Amidst the cacophony, my life didn't flash before my eyes; it screamed, raw and intense. Visions of my childhood surged forward. I saw my mother and the

Chapter 7: Amidst the Storm

resentment I felt for her decision to remain in an abusive relationship with Dick. My father's face emerged too, with his unwavering love for me. I regretted not understanding him earlier, for my anger had always clouded my judgment. I had always believed he abandoned me, but in those moments, I realized that if he had just shared his battles with me, I might've seen things differently.

Rich's face appeared next. The man I was supposed to spend the rest of my life with. But deep down, I knew my trust in him was wobbly, and our future uncertain.

As the storm raged on, I wished I had never taken the leap to move to Hawaii. Perhaps, if I had stayed, I could've finished college and steered my life on a different course.

When the hurricane's fervor finally waned, we emerged, timid and shaken, into a home no longer ours. In Hawaii, it is customary to not wear shoes inside. So, once the storm passed and it was safe to come out of the bathroom, we were barefoot. With our feet bleeding from the broken glass, we were able to see its devastation. What stood was a skeleton of memories. The roof was completely gone, and the windows shattered were monuments to a peace we once knew. Oddly, bird feathers were embedded in the walls, surreal remnants of the storm's bizarre fury. Parked cars at hotels were stacked on top of each other. Entire houses completely intact were now blocks away from where they were located on the shoreline. Our existence was now a broken landscape, a cruel mockery under the sky that betrayed us. We were powerless, with scant food, surrounded by devastation, except for one inexplicable miracle: my car. A candy apple red Fiero without a single scratch. Amidst all the wreckage, it stood unscathed, a beacon of resilience—or sheer luck—in the garage rubble.

In the days that followed, life regressed to something primal. The island smelled of rotting fish. The river became our bath, its persistent flow a subtle reminder of life's continuity. Meals, scarce as they were, became a communal rite, shared amongst survivors like a sacred offering of camaraderie and hope. Our saviors wore camouflage and heavy boots, their presence a promise of recovery and a return to civilization.

The desperation to escape the chaos of the island became overwhelming. With no feasible way to transport my car, which had miraculously remained unscathed throughout the hurricane, I made a rash decision at the airport. In a blur of anxiety and haste, I signed the title over to a complete stranger—gave the car away, and never gave it a second thought.

Our exodus to Oahu was nothing short of a refugee's journey. We waited and slept in line at the airport for several days. The island had no electricity, so the planes could only take off during daylight hours.

Aboard a B52 stripped of comfort and laden with the heavy silence of those who had lost everything. As I sat in a net seat, I remember the fog of pure oxygen as we ascended to the sky, oh how I looked forward to a glass of fresh water filled with ice.

We arrived penniless, seeking refuge in a Sheraton Hotel. My engagement ring—an emblem of love—was dismissed as worthless collateral by the hotel check-in person. She refused to help us, knowing the trauma we had just endured. I'll never forget how cruel and dismissive she was to us in our unclean clothes. Then, humanity shone through the despair: a stranger, an angel in the guise of a man behind us in line, overheard our situation and he was appalled. He spoke to the manager about how rude they were and he thought about his own kids and what would have happened to them in this situation. He paid for our room and our dinner that night. I can't remember his name now, but I will never forget his face or his kindness, and now I take that moment with me every day of my life.

Salvation extended its hand with my Dad's money, sent across the vast, indifferent sea via Western Union. Our anonymous benefactor was promptly reimbursed and we appreciatively took him to dinner. We lingered in Oahu for a week and tried to relax, the ghost of the hurricane's screams still haunting in the back of our minds.

In the aftermath, the island as all who knew it, was unrecognizable. More than 1,500 homes were ravaged, creating vulnerability where confidence once resided. Tourism, the lifeblood of the island's economy, was gutted, the paradise lost in the ruins. Yet, amidst the chaos, the spirit of 'Aloha' blossomed. Neighbors became family and the lines that often divided blurred into insignificance.

The road to recovery was not measured in days or weeks but in years. It wasn't just about rebuilding what was lost, but coming to terms with the newfound respect for nature's might. Everyone learned, adapted, and as a community, embraced a resilience that seemed woven into the very fabric of our being human.

Hurricane Iniki, while a maelstrom of devastation, was also a crucible of the human spirit. It was a testament to our ability to not only endure but to rise from the ashes, stronger and more united. This chapter of my life is not just a tale of survival, but a homage to the resilience inherent in each of us, and a recognition of the rebellious spirit that refuses to be broken even in the face of nature's fiercest storms.

CHAPTER 8:
Crossroads and New Horizons

The Essence of "If"

Touching down on the mainland, the world around me buzzed with a familiarity that now felt foreign. From Oahu to San Francisco, the journey was less about miles traveled and more about the distance I'd come within myself. Time spent with Rich's parents was a gentle balm, their gift of a new car a testament to life's persistence amidst the chaos. Yet, as we drove towards Arizona, our pit stop in Albuquerque unearthed demons I'd long buried.

In my mother's house, an innocent laundry chore upended my world. Rich, holding a cut-short straw—a harbinger of a truth I wasn't ready to face—ushered me into a storm of a different kind. He found the straw in the dryer lint tray and presented it to me. I didn't know what it was, or why the big deal. He explained that this is a straw used to snort cocaine. He would know, because he had done it many times before he met me. So, we went looking for more evidence in her house. Our search led us to a drawer, a glass mirror, white residue, and a razor blade: silent witnesses to my mother's descent from alcohol to something far more sinister. My outrage was a tempest, confrontation inevitable. But her denial, in the face of irrefutable evidence, was a dagger to my heart. Her addictions, escalating in their ferocity, were consuming her, and again I was powerless to halt their course.

The tempest of Iniki had been merciless, stripping me bare, and leaving me vulnerable to a whirlwind of insecurities and fears. The hurricane didn't just batter the island; it tore apart the trust I had in my fiancé. Every decision, every move for our safety, I took the reins. His hesitation, and his uncertainty in those crucial moments, spoke volumes to me. It became painfully clear that he couldn't protect me when it mattered most. That realization was like a second storm inside me, and by the end of it, my respect for him had been washed away with the wind and the rain.

Waves of uncertainty crashed over me, relentless and unyielding: our paths were diverging. Despite the profound attraction, the trauma we'd weathered side by side, and the idyllic days we'd spent in our island paradise, something fundamental was amiss. Trust, once shattered, defied restoration for me. I craved a love that stood resolute, unshaken by life's fiercest storms, and a man who could protect me.

Thus, with a heart laden with sorrow and eyes alight with resolve, I chose to end our relationship at a gas station on our way out of town heading back to Tucson. I don't even remember what was said, I just made the decision to get out of the car and told him I didn't want to marry him and I walked away.

Sometimes the Universe leads you not where you intended to go, but exactly where you belong. Salvation came in an unexpected guise: my Uncle Gary, now bitterly

Chapter 8: Crossroads and New Horizons

divorced from Pamela, was a real estate maestro with an astute vision for latent potential. His offer to come work for him was more than a job; it was a beacon of hope amidst my tumultuous sea.

It's said that some of the most profound influences in our lives come from unexpected quarters. For me, that influence was my Uncle Gary. While the world knew him through headlines and stories, to me, he was just an uncle, mentor, and friend—a guiding light in a time when my world was turbulent.

Working under his wing wasn't just a job; it was an immersion into life's lessons. He had this uncanny ability to transform everyday tasks into learning experiences. The wisdom he imparted went beyond the boundaries of professional work, seeping into life skills that I carry with me to this day.

One of the most vivid memories I have of my time with him is the way he taught me to type. Gary believed in the power of self-reliance and the ability to adapt to the changing world. In a time when computers were becoming household staples, he saw the importance of being adept at using them. But his teaching method was unique. He purchased a computer program designed to teach typing, a simple enough gesture. But then, he added a twist. Covering my hands with a towel, he forced me to learn the keyboard by touch alone, ensuring I wouldn't become reliant on sight. It was challenging, frustrating even, but it honed a skill in me that stands out even today. Thanks to his unconventional teaching, my fingers dance across the keyboard faster than anyone I've ever met.

But beyond the tangible skills, Gary instilled in me values that have shaped my perspective. His approach to challenges, his determination, and his unwavering belief in the potential of those around him were contagious. Every interaction was a lesson, every challenge a test of character and resolve.

Writing about my uncle isn't just about reminiscing; it's about honoring a man whose impact on my life is immeasurable. In the brief time we had together, he molded me in ways that years elsewhere never could. While the pain of his loss still stings, the gratitude for the time spent learning from him is overwhelming.

Under his tutelage, I learned more than the art of negotiation and the intricacies of development, and entrepreneurship; I discovered my own resilience. He gifted me a new perspective, teaching me to discern not only what lay before my eyes, but the possibilities that stretched out on the horizon. It was a lesson in rebirth, in crafting a future where scars were not just remnants of suffering, but badges of survival and wisdom hard-earned.

With each lesson he taught me, I rebuilt a piece of myself, molding a future rich with promise. Amidst the business dealings, I found it—the fortitude to forge ahead, to envision a life where the past was not an anchor, but a catalyst for the journey ahead.

Rudyard Kipling's "If" wasn't just a poem for Uncle Gary; it was a philosophy, a compass that he navigated life with. Whenever I think of him, the resonating words of that poem intertwine with memories, painting a clear picture of the man he was.

Every stanza of "If" seemed to mirror the values my Uncle held dear. The calm demeanor he maintained, regardless of the storms that raged around, reflected Kipling's counsel to "keep your head when all about you are losing

Chapter 8: Crossroads and New Horizons

theirs." His determination to persevere, even when faced with setbacks, was reminiscent of the line, "If you can meet with Triumph and Disaster, and treat those two impostors just the same."

Working with him, I often felt like I was living within the verses of that cherished poem. His approach to life, the grace with which he handled challenges, and the wisdom he shared all seemed to flow from the essence of Kipling's words. And in doing so, he made those words come alive for me.

The lessons from "If" were not merely recited; they were lived. The poem's call to dream yet not make dreams one's master, to think without making thoughts one's aim, found embodiment in Gary's balanced approach to ambitions and reality. His capacity to risk it all in a venture, yet start again at his beginnings when he lost, showed the courage Kipling celebrated.

Perhaps what stands out most is the poem's closing line, a culmination of all the virtues it extols: "Yours is the Earth and everything that's in it, And—which is more—you'll be a Man, my son!" Gary was not just a man in the conventional sense, but a towering figure of integrity, resilience, and wisdom.

To this day, whenever I come across "If", I don't just hear Kipling's voice; I hear my Uncle Gary. I remember the man who not only cherished those words but lived them, teaching me and many others their profound meaning through his actions.

If—

by Rudyard Kipling

If you can keep your head when all about you
   Are losing theirs and blaming it on you,
If you can trust yourself when all men doubt you,
   But make allowance for their doubting too;
If you can wait and not be tired by waiting,
   Or being lied about, don't deal in lies,
Or being hated, don't give way to hating,
   And yet don't look too good, nor talk too wise:

If you can dream—and not make dreams your master;
   If you can think—and not make thoughts your aim;
If you can meet with Triumph and Disaster
   And treat those two impostors just the same;
If you can bear to hear the truth you've spoken
   Twisted by knaves to make a trap for fools,
Or watch the things you gave your life to, broken,
   And stoop and build 'em up with worn-out tools:

If you can make one heap of all your winnings
  And risk it on one turn of pitch-and-toss,
And lose, and start again at your beginnings
  And never breathe a word about your loss;
If you can force your heart and nerve and sinew
  To serve your turn long after they are gone,
And so hold on when there is nothing in you
  Except the Will which says to them: 'Hold on!'

If you can talk with crowds and keep your virtue,
  Or walk with Kings—nor lose the common touch,
If neither foes nor loving friends can hurt you,
  If all men count with you, but none too much;
If you can fill the unforgiving minute
  With sixty seconds' worth of distance run,
Yours is the Earth and everything that's in it,
  And—which is more—you'll be a Man, my son!

CHAPTER 9:

Unveiling Shadows, Seeking Light

In late 1994 I met Roger. The setting was a lively club, the air thick with music and laughter. I was there with my cherished friend, Faydra. Roger was on the opposite side of the room, surrounded by his boisterous group of friends.

From the get-go, Roger's humor was magnetic. His jokes, his witty remarks—they sparked a laughter in me that I hadn't experienced in so long. At one point, Faydra pulled me aside, her eyes dancing with mischief. "Roger just asked if you're into him," she whispered, her giggle infectious. Before I could even reply, she blurted out, "I told him no!" Her playful denial only added to the night's unpredictable charm.

Then, in a moment straight out of a wild movie scene, one of Roger's friends burst back into the bar. Before I knew it, I was hoisted over his shoulder and deposited into the back seat of a gleaming convertible. A minute later, Faydra plopped beside me, and off we went to a party, where the night's adventures truly began.

Our night ended at a serene park. The gentle creaking of the swing set accompanied our conversations, as Roger gently pushed me back and forth. We talked, laughed, and shared stories until the stars blanketed the sky. From that night on, our bond deepened daily. Yet, for months, he never made a move to kiss me. It baffled and intrigued me. For the first time, I met someone who was genuinely interested in my soul, my laughter, and my company. With Roger, I felt safe and valued beyond the superficial. It was refreshing and healing in ways I never expected.

I thought I had finally found happiness and a sense of control in my life. I was now working for my Uncle Gary and was madly in love with Roger. I felt confident, and valued, and it seemed like my future was heading in a direction I could steer.

But life, as it always did, again tilted.

It was a beautiful day in our quiet, affluent side of town when the earth-shattering news stunned the illusion of stability. November 1, 1996, remains not just a date but a fracture in time forever.

But let me start from the night before... it had been filled with Halloween revelry. Roger and I had embraced the festive spirit, dressing up as a pair that turned heads: he was a flamboyant pimp, complete with an Afro wig, while I played the part of his beck-and-call girl, donning a striking blonde wig. At a time long before the sensitivities around blackface emerged, our costumes, though inappropriate now, went unnoticed. The true mischief of the night began when I, in my characteristic bold fashion, decided to leave the party through the entrance—a move against the party rules. As a striking young woman, I was easily forgiven. But Roger, closely following behind me wasn't so lucky. Moments later, as I looked back, I saw bouncers tackling him to the ground. A chaotic fight ensued, those who knew

Chapter 9: Unveiling Shadows, Seeking Light

Roger jumped in to help him and by the end of it, Roger had suffered a concussion.

Our next stop wasn't home, but the hospital. As the hours ticked by, I couldn't help but be aware of an impending family event: my Uncle Gary's surprise birthday party.

Lost in the hospital's sterile monotony, the shrill beeping of my pager brought me back to reality (yes, I had a pager back then). Glancing at its screen, I saw the urgency: 911, 911, 911. I quickly asked a nurse if I could use the phone and dialed the number flashing on my pager. My Aunt Mary's voice, laced with anxiety, greeted me. She delivered the shocking news she just saw on a local news station: someone had detonated a bomb in my uncle's car at La Paloma Country Club.

Disbelief and horror churned within me. Thinking it was some twisted joke, I disconnected the call. Instinctively, I dialed the nearby restaurant that we often frequented on Friday night on our way home. I asked the hostess to put the familiar bartender, a friend of our family, on the phone. He picked up. His voice, shaky and full of sorrow, said all that needed to be said, "Missy, I'm sorry. I'm so, so sorry." I was speechless. I could not formulate a sentence. Tears threatened to spill, but before they could, a whirlwind of activity surrounded me. Reporters flooded the hospital, drawn by another victim of the explosion: a caddy from the club who was injured.

In a haze, I think without even notifying Roger, I ran out of the hospital, jumped into my car, and drove straight to La Paloma, desperate to find my uncle and make sense of the inexplicable tragedy. I remember a barricade of police officers and drove right through them. An officer finally stopped me and asked me who I was, I remember throwing my driver's license and him, as I got out of my car and started running toward the tail lights of my uncle's car.

The chaos was a living entity at the scene, ATF and FBI agents everywhere. But it was Detective Jim Gamber who anchored me in the maelstrom, preventing me from witnessing the full horror of my uncle's car before I got too close to it—I don't remember much after that, other than Jim taking me into a place where we could talk and giving him the keys to the office, so he could go there search for evidence and I remember telling him that the only person who had anything to gain from his death was Pamela. His money-hungry ex-wife.

At 26, the ground beneath me cracked, leaving me perched on the precipice of an abyss that yawned wide and dark. The months that followed are a blur to me and have been ever since. I remember going home eventually and crying in my closet for what seemed to be days. I remember Roger sitting there with me. The funeral? No recollection of it at all, other than there were so many people there that they could not all enter the church so the crowd spilled out into the parking lot.

Gary was more than a prominent real estate developer in Tucson, Arizona; he was a visionary who saw potential in the arid landscapes of the desert. To me, he was Uncle Gary, my father's older brother, a larger-than-life figure whose ambition was matched only by his generosity and love of life. His untimely death at the age I am now writing this, 53, and in fact, the date I am editing this book is November 1st, 2023. As I realize this I have a lump in my throat the size of Texas and can barely breathe.

This was not just the shattering of an individual's life but the crumbling of an icon who stood for resilience and

Chapter 9: Unveiling Shadows, Seeking Light

innovation. His murder, a sinister plot involving a car bomb, for no other reason than greed, plunged me into an over decade-long hell—a harrowing maze of fear, injustice, and the relentless pursuit of truth.

In the quake's aftermath, paranoia became my shadow. Evidence emerged that Ronald Young, the architect of our tragedy, had once trailed me as prey or since I was always with my uncle at the time, followed me for information. He had notes in his car detailing my black Corvette and my license plate; MISSIE. This realization was a chill that gripped my heart, lingering as years trudged on, each laden with unspoken accusations and an intuition that screamed of Pam's involvement, yet without proof's damning finality, I didn't know for sure, so wherever I went I was suspicious of everyone around me.

It was against this backdrop of unease that I sought the counsel of a psychic. It may have been desperation or perhaps a flicker of hope that led me to her door. She had worked for the FBI in the past assisting them with unsolved crimes and finding leads for detectives. The atmosphere of her room was a stark contrast to the chaos in my mind—a serene space scented with lavender, walls lined with books and crystals that caught the light.

As soon as our eyes met, she reached for my hands, her gaze locking onto mine with an intensity that made my heart skip. "There is someone here," she began, her voice steady, "a man, large in stature. He says he's proud of the mother you are." Then, unexpectedly, she began to sing, "Why do birds suddenly appear, every time, you are near, just like me, they long to be, close to you..." Tears blurred my vision; those words were the lullaby I sang to my son each night, a private ritual of love and comfort as I rocked him to sleep.

She asked if I recognized the song, and as I nodded through my tears, she conveyed his message: "He sees you. He doesn't want you to worry." The psychic's eyes softened, and she imparted a patience I had long since lost. "The truth will come out," she assured me, "but it's not time yet. You must be patient; things don't always happen when we want them to, and often for reasons that will only make sense later."

I pleaded for more, anything that would give me a sense of direction or peace. In response, she simply began singing "Daniel" by Elton John. It was a melody that didn't fit into the puzzle of my past, yet it left an imprint that I carry with me. To this day, the song's meaning remains elusive, but as night falls and I close my eyes, I can still see the haunting glow of the red tail lights from Uncle Gary's car that fateful evening.

The psychic's words did more than offer predictions; they provided solace in a time of ultimate fear. She foretold of trials and tribulations, of truths coming to light, and of a winding path to justice—all of which, decades later, unfolded as if she had read the pages of our lives before they were written. That conversation, recorded on a now-obsolete cassette, is a testament to a moment when the veil thinned, and a message of hope reached through from beyond.

I often think about digitizing that old tape, to preserve not just the words of the psychic, but the timbre of a moment when the boundaries between here and the hereafter seemed momentarily bridged. As the years have progressed, her words have become a compass, guiding me through the fog of loss and the labyrinth of the legal system.

Almost a decade later relief came disguised as further turmoil: Ronald Young's arrest.

Chapter 9: Unveiling Shadows, Seeking Light

Nine years after the murder, on November 19, 2005, an episode of *America's Most Wanted* profiled Ronald Young, who was then wanted for forgery and embezzlement. The episode also mentioned his suspected involvement in Gary's death. Two days later, Young was apprehended in Fort Lauderdale, Florida after his chiropractor called in after seeing the show and identified him as his patient, who had an appointment coming up. He served a 10-month sentence in federal prison for weapon possession before being extradited back to Aspen, Colorado. Following Young's arrest, investigators found records of phone calls and email correspondence between Young and Pamela Phillips related to Triano's murder.

In 2008, Ronald Young was charged with the murder of my uncle. His trial was an odyssey, the courtroom a battleground where truths were both weapons and shields. It cost me and my family dearly to sit through this lengthy trial. In both precious time and it was financially exhaustive for all of us.

I remember so vividly the somber courtroom, the air was thick with anticipation as a key witness took the stand—a former cellmate of Ronald Young, the man whose hands dealt the fatal blow to my uncle. The witness recounted a haunting confession that still lingers with me like a relentless echo. He revealed how Young, with a chilling casualness, recalled the day of the murder, saying, "So I blew that motherfucker up in his car!" Those words, so vile and callous, cut through the silence of the court, sending shivers down my spine. Those brutal words and his voice still haunt my dreams to this day.

The victory was pyrrhic, and the saga was far from over. Upon his conviction, Pamela Phillips, the woman who I believed harbored venom beneath her skin all along, fled our justice for Switzerland's cold embrace. It became a waiting game, years stretching thin across diplomatic pleas and our legal swamp. Switzerland has no extradition law when a person is facing the death penalty in the United States, so even though they knew where she was—they could not bring her back.

On December 3, 2009, Pamela Phillips was finally arrested for Gary's murder in Vienna, Austria, when she fled after her indictment in October 2008. She was soon returned to the United States to stand trial.

Her extradition was not a triumph, but a deep, shuddering breath after a plunge into icy waters. Back on American soil, we waited and watched as she was escorted from the plane to the back of a police car, and I was there, not just as a witness, but as a monument to the tenacity of memory and the unyielding demand for justice. Her trial proceedings are now a blur, a deluge of testimonies, evidence, and faces worn weary by the weight of years and secrets too heavy to bear alone.

When the gavel finally fell on Pamela's fate, it was not an end, but an echo—a sound that would ripple through the remainder of my days. I remember vividly that the lights in the courtroom also flickered at that exact moment. My cousin and I locked eyes and we knew, Uncle Gary was there. Justice is not a salve, but a signpost, marking how far we've come and how much further we have yet to go. It was bittersweet. She was now going to prison, but my uncle was still physically gone. My younger cousins the 2 children she had with my uncle had no father and now no mother in their life. It was without question, a terrible zero-sum game in the end.

Chapter 9: Unveiling Shadows, Seeking Light

In the wake of those tumultuous years, fear's vice-like grip has slackened, giving way to a resilience born of trials by fire and fortified in storms. The echoes of that shattered day persist, a chorus of remembrance for all that was lost and a testament to the unyielding strength forged in the crucible of betrayal and unimaginable loss. The lesson is never to be worth more dead than alive.

Now, the chapter of uncertainty has closed, and in its place, a story of resilience and resolution writes itself. The truth, as promised, has come to light, and with it, a complex peace. Yet the melodies—the lullaby for my son, and Elton John's poignant verses—remain enshrined in my memory, forever intertwined with the image of Uncle Gary's red tail lights, a beacon of love, and the eternal promise of answers just beyond the horizon.

CHAPTER 10:

Lessons from a Dragon and a Horse

Sometimes, life's most profound lessons come not from the expected mentors but from the smallest among us. Roger and I got married in April of 1999 and my son was born in June of 2000, the year of the Dragon. He was born with what seemed to be an inconspicuous dimple on his lower back, a subtle marker that would lead us on a journey neither of us anticipated. Despite reassurances from my doctors, a mother's instinct whispered of something lurking beneath the surface. Trusting this intuition, I reached out to Dr. Harold Rekate, a renowned pediatric neurosurgeon at the Barrow Institute in Phoenix, Arizona, with nothing but a photo and a plea for help.

Tests revealed a tethered spinal cord, a silent threat that promised a future robbed of mobility, of freedom. If left unaddressed, total paralysis was a guarantee by the time his little body began to grow. Spinal cord surgery, as terrifying a prospect as it was, became our only hope.

In the aftermath, I remember staring at his small form—his arm taped to a board to stabilize the IV, his body eerily still. For days, he was awake but remained completely frozen, and a cold dread settled in my heart. Had the attempt to save his future mobility cost him his present? Yet, the moment his IV and arm board were removed by Dr. Rekate, my little boy returned to me in all his vibrant energy, smiling and giggling. Moving as though the ordeal had been nothing to him. He immediately stood up grabbed the bars on the side of his bed and started jumping up and down. Terrified he would hurt himself, I told him to lie back down, but Dr. Rekate assured me that he was fine. He said, "He has no idea that he had surgery and he has no pain because he doesn't expect any pain, and also, I'm a fantastic surgeon!"

His unbridled joy and absence of fear were a revelation—he didn't know he "should" be in pain because he had no preconceived notions of trauma. In his innocence, my son taught me about the limitations we impose on ourselves through fear and expectation. His courage wasn't just inspirational; it was transformative. This tiny titan, with his boundless spirit and unspoken strength, became my hero, imparting a lesson I would carry forth forever: the power of resilience, the chains of fear, and the healing grace of innocence. He spent the rest of his days there walking the halls and bringing cheer to all the other kids in the hospital.

Just when I thought my heart had reached its fullest capacity, life presented me with a startling revelation: I was pregnant again. The news sent waves of panic through me. How could I possibly divide the all-encompassing love I felt for my son? How could there be room in my heart for another? Yet, in July of 2022, the Year of the Horse, my daughter came into the world and promptly demolished every fear and doubt that had clouded my mind.

Chapter 10: Lessons from a Dragon and a Horse

From the first moment, I laid eyes on her—my little one who, with her endearing newborn fuzz and big, bright eyes, resembled a tiny, hairy monkey—something within me shifted profoundly. It wasn't a division of love but a multiplication; an overflow that rushed through every vein, every corner of my soul, until I thought I might burst from the sheer magnitude of it all.

My sweet Princess Buttercup Girl, in all her delicate newness, was teaching me already. She was showing me the boundless expanse of a mother's heart, the fierce resolve that had lain dormant within me, awaiting her arrival to awaken fully. From her, I learned that love isn't finite, measured, and apportioned but rather an infinite resource, capable of growing exponentially with every heartbeat.

She became my strength, my reminder that love knows no bounds, and my testament to the fact that the heart, miraculous in its elasticity, only becomes more massive when challenged to accommodate more love. In her, I discovered not just another piece of myself but an entire universe that I hadn't known existed. She didn't just fill my heart; she transformed it.

My two beautiful children, now blossoming in their early 20s, have unknowingly been my greatest teachers. Through their eyes, I've relearned life, unraveling layers of myself I never knew existed. They've flourished into honors students, their academic zeal matched only by artistic talents that defy the confines of mere imagination. Their creativity cascades boundlessly, painting their worlds with vibrant hues of ingenuity that leave me in awe.

They both faced the 2020 pandemic with a resilience and fortitude that astounded me. Amidst a world upended, they stood unflinching, navigating the uncertainties and challenges like seasoned captains steering through a storm. Their strength didn't manifest in grand gestures but in the quiet resolve, adaptability, and unwavering courage they displayed each day. They balanced caution with optimism, responsibility with hope, forging ahead when the future seemed nothing but a hazy outline. In a period that brought even the mightiest to their knees, they emerged not just unscathed but stronger, their spirits alight with the indomitable flame of youth. They didn't just endure; they thrived, and that, in itself, is nothing short of inspirational.

As I stand back and marvel at the trajectories of their lives, pride swells within me, an uncontainable tide of admiration for the remarkable individuals they've become. Their achievements are not just accolades to be admired but reflections of their inner brilliance, and for that, my heart brims with respect and endless gratitude.

CHAPTER 11:

Lessons in Humility

My career in real estate had evolved into something remarkable, and I had also transitioned into the mortgage banking industry, where I not only thrived but emerged as a leader in that field. Financially, I was making more money than I could have ever imagined. I was buying and flipping homes and I believed myself to be very successful.

Amidst the incredible wonder of raising my young son and daughter, I made a decision that brought a new sense of fulfillment. I returned to college at night to finish my business degree, a pursuit that rekindled a passion for learning I hadn't felt ever. Those late-night classes were invigorating, and I had never been happier in my entire life. It was as though the missing piece of my puzzle had been found, and I was whole.

My son and daughter were the anchors of my existence, bringing joy and purpose to every day. But, like any story, there was a shadow cast over this chapter too. Our marriage was struggling, and it was a complex tangle of emotions and insecurities that fueled the flames of discord.

The shadows of a traumatic past, particularly one punctured by broken trust, can stretch long into the heart of a marriage, warping perspectives and seeding doubts. I recall, with clarity touched by the cold fingers of fear, the moment that marked a turning point for me. It was an ordinary day, with Roger engaged in a mundane task: selling a Honda Accord. The buyer, an unremarkable girl, was the unlikely catalyst for the resurgence of my deep-seated insecurities. As I observed them from our home's window, the innocuous scene twisted before me. Her laughter seemed flirtatious, her gaze lingered too long, and the scenario stoked ancient fears, awakening old but potent anxieties about abandonment and unworthiness.

It wasn't just jealousy that clenched my heart; it was a sudden, crippling realization of my own vulnerability. I was starkly reminded of the imperative to protect myself, to be self-sufficient because the haunting narrative etched into my psyche since childhood whispered insidiously that it wasn't a question of if he would leave me, but when. This moment, seemingly trivial to any passerby, ignited a fear that would become a constant, unwelcome companion in my life. It propelled me back into the workforce, not as a pursuit of personal fulfillment, but as a lifeboat against a future tidal wave of betrayal and abandonment that my past had convinced me was inevitable.

As time marched on, with the psychic's words etched into the backdrop of my reality, life demanded a semblance of normalcy. I immersed myself back into the workforce, driven perhaps by a need to find grounding in the tangible. Success, it seemed, was waiting for me with open arms.

This success, however, was a double-edged sword. It afforded Roger and me a fantastic lifestyle, one of comfort

Chapter 11: Lessons in Humility

and luxury that we were both so grateful for. Yet, I could see the weight of our reversed roles pressing down upon him. Roger, ever the strong, leader type, took on the mantle of parenting with a grace that belied his internal struggle. As I stepped into the larger role of provider, I inadvertently challenged the traditional image he held of masculinity.

It wasn't the life he had envisioned for us, nor mine initially, but the glint of sadness in his eyes spoke volumes of the depression that was silently setting in. I understood this; I empathized. But empathy was a silent partner to my own inability to express vulnerability—a trait that often left me armored against the very intimacy that could have likely bridged our growing divide.

Strong we both were, Roger and I, but in that strength lay our common weakness: an unspoken battle of pride and expectation versus the reality of our shifting world. I could not help but wonder if the psychic's assurances, the patient unraveling of the universe's plan, applied not only to the mysteries of the past but also to the intimate intricacies of our present lives.

While our marriage wavered under the weight of silent struggles, maintaining a façade of normalcy as I juggled relentless work hours with dedicated parenting, it was not his actions but a deeply buried secret of mine that ultimately steered us toward the precipice of divorce, a truth I could never muster the courage to reveal to him.

Success, often portrayed as a panacea, couldn't shield me from the unforeseen storm that approached on an otherwise not particularly interesting business trip. Amidst the deceptive safety of camaraderie, laughter, and drinks, a trusted employee one that I brought into this business and trained, and a long-time family friend—a label that would soon feel bitterly ironic—accompanied me on the hotel elevator, his intentions shrouded in the haze of alcohol that clouded us both. The sanctuary of my room became the setting of my violation when, with the door barely closed, I was shoved inside and assaulted within moments. Before I could even grapple with the reality of what transpired, he disappeared, leaving me alone with my turmoil, tears merging with the silent scream of betrayal. I didn't even know something like that could happen in under 2 min!

Adrift in shock, I cocooned the incident within the recesses of my mind, masquerading it as an outrageous nightmare, its sharp edges too brutal for daylight. I took a shower and I cried myself to sleep.

The silence felt like my only refuge because admitting the truth was to acknowledge my own unexpected fragility, a contradiction to the strength I had always projected. But silence has its own echoes, and they reverberated deafeningly when, in a cruel twist, on the following Monday, he attempted to undermine my reputation before abruptly resigning. His fabrications about racism, absurd to anyone aware of my Hispanic heritage, were a transparent smokescreen to preemptively protect himself, revealing the cowardice that lurked beneath his opportunism. Luckily, HR disregarded his absurd and lack of any substance remarks and they bid him farewell.

This episode wasn't just an assault on my physical being but an insidious theft of trust and a stark lesson in the unpredictability of human nature. It underscored the bitter truth that vulnerability can find us even when we feel strongest, and that our own perceptions of strength and weakness are, in fact, not as we imagine them to be. The experience etched a painful but crucial understanding deep

Chapter 11: Lessons in Humility

within me: that strength isn't defined by an absence of vulnerability, but by the courage to continue and the resilience to rebuild, even from the darkest moments.

Our marriage ended swiftly, concluding in just 30 days. We made an arrangement that granted me full custody of our children, and in exchange for not paying him alimony, he was freed from the obligation of child support. Surprisingly, the separation was amicable, and we even embarked on a cruise with our kids shortly afterward, trying to maintain a sense of normalcy for their sake and we genuinely enjoyed each other's company. He was my best friend. Yet, I could never share this horrible night with him and you must understand that holding a secret for me is impossible. If I had told him, he would have killed him and more importantly it would have broken his heart. I could not do that at the time. So, I ended it.

A few short months later in 2007, the market crashed, and the financial foundation I had built crumbled like a house of cards. Overnight, my income plummeted by a staggering 60%, and the properties I owned were suddenly upside down, their values sinking like stones in water. It was a harsh wake-up call, a reminder of my own arrogance and misplaced priorities.

I had erroneously placed my self-worth on my career success, and when that success vanished, I was left with a profound sense of fear and insecurity. Sticky notes bearing my visions and goals adorned every surface of my life, and my entire team knew my lofty ambition: to achieve 100% debt-free status by the time I turned 40.

Ironically, on my 40th birthday, I did indeed reach that goal, but not in the triumphant manner I had envisioned. My bankruptcy was finalized, and I was officially debt-free exactly the day before. It was a bitter irony, a lesson in the importance of being specific with your manifestations.

The experience was humbling, to say the least. It taught me that true success isn't solely measured by financial accomplishments or material possessions. It's about resilience, adaptability, and the ability to confront life's curveballs head-on. I had to rebuild not only my financial stability but also my sense of self-worth and priorities. It was a period of reflection, growth, and ultimately, a deeper understanding of what truly matters in life. Still, I felt like a huge failure and I indeed was in many ways.

CHAPTER 12:

From Darkness to Dawn

A Journey of Struggle and Hope

In the wake of my bankruptcy and the sudden upheaval of my financial stability, I found myself lost and adrift in a sea of uncertainty. Instead of facing my challenges head-on, I chose a different path, one that led me further into darkness. I turned to drinking as a coping mechanism, seeking solace at the bottom of a wine bottle.

The consequences of my choices began to manifest in my children's lives as well. They had been attending private school, a choice I could no longer afford. As my financial situation deteriorated, I watched helplessly as the educational opportunities I had once provided for them slipped through my fingers and now fell into the hands of their father.

Meanwhile, the trial for my uncle's murder loomed on the horizon, casting a long shadow over my life. It would become a protracted legal battle that stretched on for years, demanding my time, attention, and emotional energy. In an effort to protect my children from the turmoil surrounding the trial and the uncertainty in my own life, I made a painful decision. I allowed their father to have them most of the time, providing them with stability and consistency, as my own life unraveled. I never liked bouncing between my parent's houses and I didn't want them to be disheveled like I was as a kid. It made sense in my mind and also, and I also knew how much Roger loved and needed to be with them. He by then, had his own business and could more easily work his schedule around pick up and drop-offs during the school week. So, it seemed to make logical sense.

As the months turned into years, I spiraled deeper into my own darkness. The weight of my choices, the pain over not being with my children as I once had, and the overwhelming burden of the trial took its toll on my mental and emotional well-being. It was a period of profound struggle and despair, a descent into a darkness that seemed all-consuming.

In the shadows of my life's most tempestuous chapter, fate steered Steve back into my orbit in 2010. We had actually met briefly when I was in high school though I did not yet live in Arizona, only visiting at the time, we never saw each other again. Plus, at that time I thought he was way too tall!

This time we collided, two souls ravaged by time and tumultuous pasts, and tumbled headfirst into a love so profound it bordered on the maddening. Now both of us divorced with kids, we were kindred spirits wrestling with our private demons. Our chemistry was undeniable, a magnetic pull that rendered us inseparable. However, in the refuge, we sought in each other, we also found escape in the numbing embrace of alcohol, a crutch that was far from a stranger to either of us.

Chapter 12: From Darkness to Dawn

Our liquid courage, rather than being our salve, unearthed the worst in us. Steve, with every drink, metamorphosed into a version of himself that teetered on the edge, his anger and jealousy an echoing reminder of his own past wounds. I, buoyed by my innate sociability, flirted and laughed, unwittingly stoking the fires of his insecurities, mirroring the ghost of his past grievances.

Steve and I were both struggling to endure the pain of divorce. Both of us had experienced the dissolution of what we once believed were lifelong partnerships, and the aftermath was a daily struggle. We found ourselves grappling with the void left by our once-intact families. Our children, still young, faced the daunting task of navigating the fractured landscapes of split homes. Enduring this upheaval was, without exaggeration, the most harrowing challenge I had faced, surpassing all my prior tribulations by far.

The profound sadness that enveloped us was not just about our lost loves; it was about the everyday moments—preparing meals, tucking our children into bed, celebrating holidays—that we once took for granted. These times, once filled with so much joy, now felt tainted by a pervasive sense of loss. Despite the love Steve and I shared, there was an undeniable yearning for the life we once led, a life we had each willingly relinquished. Holidays especially became a stark reminder of what had been fragmented, a source of anguish where there was once unbridled happiness.

The truth is, Steve and I would give anything to turn back the hands of time, to avoid the path that led us away from the other parent of our children. Through my own experience, I implore those who come to me for counsel—to find a way to make it work. If your marriage involves children, muster every ounce of effort to preserve that union.

I cannot stress this enough, regardless of how others may portray the aftermath of their divorces, nothing compares to the devastation it brings to both the parents and the children involved. The pain and separation cut deeply, more profoundly than one can ever anticipate.

I offer this not as a judgment, but as heartfelt advice borne from a place of deep regret: unless you or your children are in danger, fight for your marriage with everything you have. The alternative is a path fraught with neverending pain, a path I would not wish upon anyone. Please, trust me on this. The cost is too great, the damage too enduring.

The nadir came crashing down on us one frigid night near Christmas. Echoes of joyous festivities still lingered in the air as we returned from a party, the warmth of my wine and his scotch veiling our senses. What sparked the argument has since been lost, overshadowed by the intensity of what followed. Our home became a battleground, words like daggers thrown without thought, the cacophony of our fury a terrifying lullaby for the children we'd forgotten were nestled in their beds.

The confrontation escalated, a terrifying resonance with the shadows of my own childhood I'd vowed never to revisit. Yet, here I was, entrenched in a war of harsh loud words and slamming doors, with a man lost in his intoxication. Logic dictated silence, a retreat, but my own fury roared louder. I was incensed, both at the disruption and the fear we were instilling in our children.

My son's tear-streaked face was my breaking point. He begged me to leave. My kids had never seen or heard anyone argue before, so they were absolutely terrified. Fueled by a protective instinct, I took my children into the car, their small bodies trembling in their pajamas, not just from

Chapter 12: From Darkness to Dawn

the cold but from the raw fear that palpable anger induces in the innocent. As we sat there, the car a haven in the frosty night, Steve emerged, remorse painting his features. But it was too late—the sirens wailed as they pulled up behind us, the flashing lights a harbinger of a nightmare I hadn't foreseen. Steve's son had been on the phone with his mother and she overheard the arguing. In an attempt to protect me, she called the police and reported domestic violence.

Their presence was an unwelcome twist in an already spiraling narrative. I explained to them what had happened and admitted having had a glass of wine at a party a couple of hours prior. Despite the turmoil, I was coherent—not drunk—though had been crying and my compliance during the field sobriety test should have proven that. However, Arizona's laws had other plans in store for me. My refusal to submit to a blood test—a reaction born from indignation, considering I was the presumed victim in this scenario—was met with a zero-tolerance response. In an instant, I was no longer a frightened mother trying to protect her children; I became a suspect, my rights slipping through my fingers as the handcuffs clicked shut around my wrists.

They took me away and left all the kids there with Steve! I was beside myself with fear and frustration. Their protocol was indifferent to my pleas, insisting that I had been drinking and driving with my children in the car! The flashing lights of the squad car were a fading promise of the justice I thought I'd have. My children, the ones I'd been trying to shield, were left behind in total confusion, an ache in my heart that throbbed with each mile that stretched between us. The irony was a bitter pill to swallow; I was ensnared by the very system I believed would protect us. Also, how this situation unfolded perplexed me. In all the years of my mother's abuse, not once did the police take either of them away! They would come and ask my mother if she wanted to press charges and she would always say no and they would just get back in their squad cars and go away, so I also had little respect for them. In fact, I remember when they put those handcuffs on me, I pulled my wrists right out and threw them at the police officer! I don't recommend this to anyone as it certainly didn't help my situation.

From the respectability of a recent Mrs. Southern Arizona, a community role model and a person who had never and would never intentionally hurt a living soul, I was thrust into the cold anonymity of a jail cell. A concrete bed and a metal toilet would be my only companion for the next 30-plus hours. The hours crawled, marked only by the echo of distant cries in my heart and the stark realization of the situation's absurdity. My crime? Defending my dignity and safeguarding my children, yet the law saw it differently—a refusal that equated to presumed guilt. Of course, they got a warrant from a judge that night to take my blood without my consent, which would later prove that I was not intoxicated, but those results would take months to come back.

The one call I made that night from the jail, wasn't for legal aid or reassurance; it was a desperate plea to their father, ensuring my children were plucked from the night's emotional wreckage. My release the next day was met by Steve waiting in the car to pick me up. Tears streamed down his face with utter remorse for the inconceivable happenings of the night before. He took me home and I slept for what felt like days.

But the journey of mending the fractured trust with our children and family was a path strewn with thorns. They forgave but the disappointment lingered, a silent specter in

Chapter 12: From Darkness to Dawn

their smiles. No one could ever understand how I could stay in this relationship, no matter what changes were made. It's a heartache that reverberates in the quiet moments, a lesson seared into my soul. I know I should have sat down and talked to them more about it, but in my embarrassment and shame and the young age the kids were, I mostly tried to cast it aside.

Through this, I learned more about what my own mother must have been experiencing. A perspective I had never been able to consider before and it made my heart break even more for her. The human heart is a curious thing. It endures pain, learns to heal, and has an uncanny ability to find love even in the midst of chaos. When I met Steve, it felt like the universe was presenting me with another test. Here was a man who, on the one hand, made my heart flutter with joy, and on the other, awakened ghosts from my past that I thought I had laid to rest.

This drinking was a storm cloud that often hung heavily over our relationship for a time. Each time I smelled alcohol on his breath, memories of my tumultuous childhood resurfaced, and fear would grip my heart. Would history repeat itself? Would I become a mirror image of my mother, a bitter victim of another man's fury? Each bout of anger, every harsh word, was like a sharp needle poking old wounds.

Yet, in the sober light of day, Steve was very different. He was the man who held my hand during tough times, who made me laugh until tears streamed down my face, and who stood by me when the world felt like a lonely place. I saw in him a battle between the man he was and the man he wanted to be. And so, I chose to go back to him, to fight alongside him, to weather this storm together.

The legal entanglements unraveled with time and finally went away, but the emotional knots that tightened around my heart remained. I moved out for about a year and Steve recognized the pain this was causing to our entire family and made the difficult decision to quit drinking. It wasn't easy for him, he lost most of his friends in this purge, but his commitment to our relationship, the desire to become a role model for the kids, and his personal growth with anger management were evident. Sobriety wasn't just a choice; it was our salvation, a pact to never revisit the darkness that had so nearly consumed our family.

We both made mistakes, as everyone does, but instead of letting them define us, we used them as stepping stones to build a stronger foundation for our relationship.

My decision to go back to him was met with raised eyebrows and concerned whispers. Friends and family struggled to understand, but how could they? They hadn't walked in my shoes, hadn't faced the monsters from my past. To them, leaving seemed the obvious choice. A zero-tolerance policy from the strong women and men in my life. But life had taught me that things were rarely black and white. I had seen the very worst that people could do, and in comparison, Steve's actions felt like ripples in a pond, not the tidal waves I had previously witnessed.

It was my stepmother's unwavering spirit and her lessons on forgiveness that kept me grounded. She had faced life's tempests head-on, teaching me the value of resilience and the power of love. I believed in Steve, in the goodness that lay beneath the surface, overshadowed by the dark veil of alcohol.

I firmly believe, now more than ever, that alcohol clouds judgment and fuels the fires of violence and depression.

Chapter 12: From Darkness to Dawn

In its absence, Steve and I have discovered a bond that's pretty unbreakable, built on understanding, and an unwavering commitment to each other. Through thick and thin, we've weathered many storms together, emerging stronger and more connected with each passing day.

In sharing this, I strip bare my lowest ebb, not to dwell in self-pity, but to embrace the vulnerability that makes us intrinsically human. It's a painful testament to the unintended consequences our actions can reap, and a reminder that sometimes, the systems meant to protect us can also fail us profoundly.

During these arduous times, I found myself estranged from my own identity and the aspirations I once embraced. Anger towards God and life itself festered within me, an anger so pervasive that it clouded my vision. I was embittered by the tragedies that lay beyond my grasp, losing sight of the very things within my power to shape. It was through this tumultuous time that I came to understand the corrosive nature of self-destructive tendencies and the profound effect they wield, not just upon oneself but also upon the cherished circle of our loved ones. Yet, amidst the shadow of despair, a stubborn spark of hope endured, nurturing a slow but steadfast journey towards redemption, a journey marked by forgiveness and a profound journey inward to the core of my being.

CHAPTER 13:

Confrontation and Catharsis

The Delicate Dance of Forgiveness

In the pursuit of rebuilding my career and transitioning into the world of medical sales and consulting for healthcare professionals, I discovered a newfound sense of purpose and satisfaction. It was a path that allowed me to assist doctors in understanding the intricate dynamics of the business side of their practice, enabling them to optimize their earnings while focusing on patient care. Life appeared to be taking a positive turn, and I basked in the joy of making a tangible impact on the lives of others.

A few years later, life had more twists and turns to unveil. Through a colossal acquisition by another formidable medical distribution conglomerate, I found myself thrust into the unpredictable turbulence of corporate reshuffling, leading to an unexpected layoff. It was a stark reminder of the capricious nature of one's professional journey. In response to this abrupt shift, I found refuge in the familiar territory of real estate and mortgage banking, although it had undergone significant transformations since the market crash.

The mind's capacity for self-preservation can be astonishing, weaving fictions so convincing that they seamlessly blend with reality. I had buried the trauma of that night in the hotel years ago so deeply, wrapping it in the guise of a nightmare, that it dissolved into the subconscious, sparing me the daily torment of its memory. This delicate tapestry of denial remained unchallenged until fate, with its unpredictable weave, brought us back into each other's professional orbits. His presence, an unexpected specter from a past I had reconfigured, threatened to unravel the seams of the protective world my psyche had constructed.

The dinner where I was heralded back into the financial industry, meant to be a celebration of new beginnings, morphed into a crucible of confrontation and catharsis.

As he sat across the table from me that night, I didn't even recall that awful night so many years ago. I fully convinced myself that it did not really happen. That it was only a terrible dream. I only knew that they had hired me for this role to build up the company in specific markets and I was very excited about this new opportunity because they told me he was there and they were quite frankly looking to replace him. So while I didn't particularly like him anymore—I would only be working with him for a short time.

It wasn't until everyone else left dinner that evening that he requested a private moment alone with me. I resettled in my seat, and before I could say anything, tears began streaming down his face. With a quivering voice, he brought up that night and apologized for his actions during that business trip, expressing profound guilt and remorse for exploiting me. He said, "I raped you". He also conveyed regret for his subsequent attempts to tarnish my reputation, revealing that his resignation was an escape because he lacked the courage

Chapter 13: Confrontation and Catharsis

to face me and apologize sooner and he was worried I would have him arrested. His confession shattered my internal defenses; the harrowing event I had tried to suppress, convincing myself it was merely a terrible nightmare, was now undeniably real. The weight of this reality was overwhelming. Yet, amidst the turmoil, I found a shred of solace in his genuine remorse and acceptance of responsibility.

His tears and apology were as unforeseen as they were unsettling, reopening a chapter I had completely blocked out of my memory. Yet, in the maelstrom of emotions that his confession unleashed—anger, confusion, a resurgence of betrayal—there too emerged an unexpected impulse to forgive.

In fact, as I recall, Dick my mother's ex—a somber echo from my childhood, called me at my office just a few weeks later. When the phone rang that day, and I heard his voice on the other end, I was transported back to those days of fear and helplessness, witnessing the violence he inflicted upon my mother. The coincidence was as startling as it was painful—two men from different chapters of my life reaching out in attempts to mend the hurt they had caused. Dick's voice, tinged with regret and the sobriety of his later years, apologized for the anguish he had caused. While I appreciated his effort to make amends, I stood firm in my resolve; some wounds were too deep to be healed by words alone. I wished him peace, but I also asked him to never contact me again. His death not long after didn't bring me joy, but it did bring a complex sense of closure. His passing was a quiet footnote to the chapters of my life he had once darkly inked, an endnote that allowed me to turn the page with a bittersweet finality.

To those who have crossed the line into harming another, know this—

acknowledgment and apology can be a powerful salve. It was years later when one of my assailants sought me out, his words heavy with genuine remorse, offering a simple, yet profound, "I'm sorry." That moment of owning up to his past unacceptable behavior, his effort to make amends, resonated deeply. It mattered.

It matters not just for the relief it brings, but for the validation it provides to the one who has suffered. Hearing the words "I'm sorry, please forgive me," can be a step towards healing, a sign that our pain is seen, and our boundaries respected. It matters that the person who wronged us strives to better themselves, to unequivocally renounce such acts, and to fully grasp the extent of the pain they caused.

To anyone who has inflicted pain, whether through carelessness or a moment of malice, understand the magnitude of your actions and take the courageous step to make amends. Your remorse, when accompanied by an unwavering commitment to change, can unlock a path to forgiveness and pave the way for healing. It won't undo the past, but it can transform the future.

And to the ones who bear the scars, know that your pain is valid, and your call for acknowledgment is just. It's not just about the apology—it's about the sincerity behind it, the promise of reformation, and the actions taken to right the wrongs. This is a message to both the wounded and the repentant: accountability matters, healing is possible, and your story deserves the dignity of recognition.

Forgiveness, I discovered, wasn't a neatly packaged decision, nor was it a reflection of weakness or an absolution of heinous actions. It was, instead, a complex dance between power and vulnerability, a reclaiming of the control that had been wrested from me those fateful nights. By granting them forgiveness, I wasn't condoning their actions or erasing their impact. Rather, I was releasing myself from the heavy chains of resentment and victimhood that, unbeknownst to me, had lingered in the shadowy corners of my consciousness. To this day, I grapple with the "why" of my forgiveness, but perhaps it was my soul's instinctive reach for freedom and healing, an acknowledgment that while the past is immutable, my response to it—my journey forward—remains firmly within my grasp.

CHAPTER 14:

Echoes of Deception

Unveiling a Hidden Truth

About a year or so later, while enjoying dinner with a close friend Jessica, on my way home from the office, a man from my past in the realm of medical sales and pharmaceutical supplies made an unexpected appearance. I considered him a friend and I had enjoyed hearing his perspectives in the industry. I was aware of his once-spoken attraction to me, a sentiment I had encountered from numerous individuals before. However, my feelings didn't align, and the substantial age difference between us further solidified our platonic relationship. I regarded him as a mentor and professional acquaintance, he reminded me of my Grandfather my mother's father in many ways, not suspecting at all the shadows lurking beneath his deceptive surface.

During our dinner conversation, I told him how I was engaged to Steve, that our wedding was in two weeks and I was moving back in with him the very next day. He asked if I was still a Physician Consultant and I told him what happened and that I had returned to real estate and my contemplation of establishing a real estate photography company. In response, he revealed that he was in the process of selling his house and suggested that I visit to assess its potential on my way home. I agreed, since it was right around the corner and I followed him there.

As I explored the property, attentively examining its features, he graciously offered a glass of ice water infused with a slice of lemon. I recollect every detail vividly, from the subtle aroma of the lemon to the play of moonlight reflecting on the pool out back. The visit was characterized by normalcy and professionalism, right up until the moment I decided it was time to bid my farewells.

The transition from leaving the house to my bewildering awakening the following morning remains a perplexing blur in my memory. I regained consciousness in a state of utter vulnerability, sprawled naked upon his bed. My immediate surroundings were alien, and my mind raced in a desperate attempt to make sense of the situation. I noticed the shattered remains of my necklace strewn upon the floor alongside my disheveled clothing. On the nightstand, I saw the most gigantic dildo I had ever seen in my life and some sort of rope-like object. Panic and terror enveloped me as I struggled to comprehend the harrowing turn of events. I had zero recollection of anything after walking towards my purse. My knee throbbed painfully as I got up and walked to the bathroom, and upon inspecting my reflection in the bathroom mirror, I discovered a bloodied, broken nose and mascara smeared across my face. Clearly I had been crying.

The sight was both horrifying and bewildering, leaving me grappling with a profound sense of violation and unsafety. My hasty efforts to retrieve my belongings and flee from the scene were fraught with fear and disorientation.

Chapter 14: Echoes of Deception

He appeared at the doorway, his demeanor disturbingly nonchalant, as if the previous night's events were inconsequential. He casually suggested that I have a nice day.

Overwhelmed by fear, confusion, and self-doubt, I made a beeline for the hospital, where a battery of tests was conducted in an attempt to unravel the mysteries of that harrowing night. The hospital notified the Sheriff's department and they introduced an unsettling dimension to my ordeal, as I recounted the events to them in painstaking detail. Despite the compelling evidence pointing to a possible assault, I grappled with the daunting notion, unable to fully accept the horrifying truth. Still, no matter what—this time, I could not stay quiet.

After piecing together fragments of the preceding night, a hazy tapestry wrought from the recesses of my memory, the doctors and police gently suggested conducting a Sexual Assault (SA) kit. Their proposition, presented with a blend of professionalism and empathy, was aimed at ruling out any foul play during the obscured hours of my unconsciousness. The very notion felt surreal, the possibility of such violation lurking in the shadowed corners of improbability. He was my friend and he was so old!!

Yet, I acquiesced, the gravity of the unknown anchoring me to a harsh reality I hadn't considered until that moment, despite the clear evidence in that room. It was inconceivable to me that something like that could happen and that I would not remember a single thing.

In the sterile silence of the examination room, amidst the clinical precision of the procedure, I found myself grappling with a disquieting thought—the realm of what I believed to be impossible had suddenly, and terrifyingly, expanded. The nurse said she had never seen so many injuries in a rape victim.

A sexual assault kit, also known as a rape kit or sexual assault forensic evidence (SAFE) kit, is a package of items used by medical professionals to collect and preserve physical evidence following allegations of sexual assault. The purpose of the kit is to gather any evidence that could be used in criminal proceedings, while also providing necessary medical care to the victim. In many states, a potential victim can have this done and still choose to not report a crime. However, it is kept for future comparison should another victim ever turn up with similar DNA findings in order to tie crimes together with a specific perpetrator. If you are ever in this situation, please ask what your state's policy is on this, as it most certainly matters if you wish to avoid a legal battle in those initial days that follow.

Here's what the process typically involves, though again, it can vary depending on the location and specific circumstances. Because this is a big topic people want to know about when I have done speaking engagements:

1. **Consent:** Before the examination, the healthcare professional will explain the process to the victim and obtain their consent. The victim has the right to accept or decline any part of the exam.
2. **Documentation of Medical History:** This includes the victim's general health, recent sexual activity, and details about the assault, such as time, location, and nature of the sexual assault.
3. **Physical Examination:** This comprehensive exam checks for and documents any physical injuries, such as bruises, lacerations, or signs of trauma. This can include an examination of the mouth, vagina, and/or anus, depending on

the nature of the alleged assault. It also includes photographs.
4. **Evidence Collection:** Using the sexual assault kit, the healthcare professional will collect evidence from the victim's body, clothing, and other personal belongings. This might include blood, saliva, semen, hair, or fibers. The specific process for collecting evidence will depend on the nature of the assault and the amount of time that has passed since it occurred.
5. **Treatment:** After the examination and evidence collection, the healthcare provider may offer preventative vaccine injections to prevent sexually transmitted infections (STIs), provide emergency contraception to prevent pregnancy, and address any other physical injuries.
6. **Follow-Up Care:** The healthcare professional might recommend follow-up appointments for additional healthcare services and provide referrals for counseling or support services.
7. **Evidence Handling:** Collected evidence is carefully packaged and preserved to prevent contamination. The kit is then handed over to law enforcement (with the victim's consent) and may be used in the investigation and prosecution of the crime.

It's important to note that the process can be emotionally and physically challenging for survivors of sexual assault. Medical professionals who carry out these exams are trained to approach the situation with sensitivity, empathy, and care to minimize any additional trauma to the victim. Also, the choice to undergo a sexual assault forensic exam is entirely up to the survivor, and their rights and choices are a priority throughout the process.

The dim lights of the hospital faded into the darkness as Steve and I headed home, the sanctuary of our own walls awaiting, yet offering no true reprieve from the day's revelations. The hushed drive was punctuated only by the sound of the phone call for takeout, an attempt at normalcy that fell flat against the backdrop of a life that abruptly capsized. Dinner lay forgotten, an afterthought in the face of a mind preoccupied with the dread of potential illness and the invisible wounds that no meal could mend.

As the valium they administered coursed through me, it was a poor balm for the turmoil that wrestled within. The doctors' words echoed, a refrain of 'retest in six months' to make sure I didn't contract AIDS, a six-month sentence of uncertainty. They also referred me to a neurologist for more tests to make sure I did not have a neurological condition that would have caused me to black out that night. My body bore the evidence of betrayal, yet my mind reeled in denial, grappling with the incongruity of the man I had known and the actions I could not reconcile. The night enveloped us in its embrace, a shroud that could not obscure the stark reality that was beginning to seep into my consciousness—the realization of the violation, the loss of trust, and the long, uncertain road to recovery that lay ahead.

CHAPTER 15:

A Battle for Justice

A Cautionary Tale

The police came to my house later that same night and asked me to call him and ask him what happened that night, so they could record his responses. I did and he maintained that he did not touch me, that I could trust him, and that he did not know how I could have broken my nose or injured my knee, that I must have fallen and gone to bed in his room. He maintained that I was alone there by myself and at no time did he ever touch me. That I could certainly trust him. That I should know that.

The morning after this surreal day, law enforcement swiftly swung into action, raiding his residence. As they combed through the house, they unearthed a grim tableau that eerily echoed my fragmented recollections. Blood stains tarnished the bed, a dark testament to the ordeal I'd suffered. Hidden within the depths of a filing cabinet in his master closet were the ropes and the grotesque dildo I'd vividly recalled seeing on the nightstand, artifacts that hinted at the depths of his depravity. And there, too, was the water glass

I'd described, its seemingly innocent contents now suspect. With every piece of evidence uncovered, the gravity of the situation became more palpable, drawing a stark picture of the nightmarish reality I'd endured.

They took it to a Grand Jury and the subsequent indictment was swift and damning. Based on the undeniable evidence and my testimony, he faced a slew of charges: unlawfully administering narcotics, kidnapping, assault with temporary disfigurement, sexual assault, sexual abuse, and aggravated assault. As I processed the mounting evidence, a maelstrom of emotions swirled within me—relief, vindication, dread, and a burning desire for justice. The path to holding him accountable had been paved.

And my life took a nightmarish turn as the well-connected prominent figure in the pharmacy world, thrust me into a maelstrom of legal battles and public shame. He was an influential individual, known for his authoritative book on pharmacoeconomics. Backed by a formidable team of six attorneys, they immediately waged a relentless assault on my character, orchestrating a public smear campaign that devastated my reputation and wreaked havoc on my professional life.

They swiftly convened a press conference, proclaiming his charges to be baseless and framing the victim as someone with an extensive criminal background and financial struggles. They posited that these allegations were fabricated, a ploy designed for monetary gain—an accusation of extortion rather than an account of victimhood.

Their tactics were ruthless and unrelenting. Lies and falsehoods were weaponized in a press conference, the very platform that should have been dedicated to truth and justice. I watched helplessly as my reputation was dragged

Chapter 15: A Battle for Justice

through the mud, my business crumbling under the weight of false accusations and misrepresentation.

They discovered my bankruptcy years prior and assumed that meant I needed money and they used the fact that I had been arrested for that DUI with my kids in the car as a basis for making these statements—never mind the fact that those charges were dismissed because I was found not to have been intoxicated, or that I had security clearance for my financial licenses and real estate licenses proving the contrary!

Employees abandoned ship finding it difficult to understand how the news would ever lie and those who did believe me had spouses who didn't know me and they naturally had their concerns, and I was left with the crushing weight of humiliation and despair.

I summoned every ounce of strength to continue showing up for work, but the shame and anger that accompanied me to the office each day were suffocating. My fury was exacerbated by the criminal court case, an arena in which I had no control. I was a victim in their case and that was all I was. A quasi-witness to their case against him. The results of the SA kit, which held the key to unlocking the truth, remained a frustrating mystery for half a year.

Backlog in Rape Kit Processing in Phoenix, Arizona

According to the most recent news article I could find; There is a significant delay in processing rape kits within the Phoenix Police Department, with hundreds of kits still awaiting testing. As a matter of fact, as of July 31st, 2023, 835 untested sex assault kits were reported.

The reason for this backlog primarily stems from a severe staff shortage in the department, a challenge many law enforcement agencies nationwide are grappling with. The Phoenix Police Department is actively hiring forensic scientists and aims to fill several vacancies in the coming months.

Of the untested kits, 300 have been sent to an external lab for testing, but the remaining 500+ kits remain unprocessed. The department plans to address this issue within the next six months, having drafted a plan to send the backlogged Sexual Assault Kits (SAKs) to external companies for processing. Kits that are deemed critical to public safety are given priority and are processed as soon as possible, usually in-house.

The law mandates the testing of every sexual assault kit, even if they pertain to already closed cases or cases where the kit might not solve the crime. Outsourcing is further complicated as the companies Phoenix Police Department relies on are also serving multiple agencies nationwide. These companies have a limit on the number of kits they can accept from the department each month.

"Christa Lindsay, from the Arizona Coalition to End Sexual and Domestic Violence, expressed concern about the negative message this delay sends to survivors. She believes that the wait adds to their trauma, emphasizing that survivors deserve to know the next steps and need closure".
—Ya think?

Governor Katie Hobbs, reflecting on her past efforts in the Senate to clear the rape kit backlog, expressed her commitment to work with law enforcement and legislators to address this recurring issue and ensure justice for victims in Arizona. But, I can tell you that this has been an issue for the past decade and still, no progress has been made.

Chapter 15: A Battle for Justice

Meanwhile, the creepy rapist's team of attorneys launched a relentless campaign of harassment against me, contacting everyone I had ever known, interrogating them, spreading lies, and leaving me feeling defenseless violated, and weak. Throughout this entire process, I was the one being treated like the villain. I was the one who had to defend myself.

In the face of this onslaught, and genuine anger, I made a pivotal decision. I retained an attorney to initiate a civil lawsuit against them all, the rapist and his attorneys, seeking justice for the devastation they had wrought upon my life and in an effort to get them to stop harassing me and my integrity.

I received the test results about 6 months later, (which was actually rushed compared to how long it takes most victims to get these tests back) and had clear undisputed evidence of being drugged to a perilous extent with a commonly prescribed drug Ambien, and they found his DNA inexplicably present all over my body (Contrary to his initial recorded statements). I was absolutely mortified and I was furious beyond measure.

So I sued the bastard for a litany of charges, including unlawfully administering narcotics, kidnapping, assault with temporary disfigurement, and sexual assault. All the same charges, he was indicted for in the criminal case and defamation of character, and in that defamation charge, I included all of his attorneys.

Despite this shocking evidence and a recorded call between me and him in which he vehemently denied any wrongdoing, the criminal case seemed to languish. His powerful influence appeared to extend even to the prosecutor's office, leading us to suspect foul play. They said, because I was unconscious and there were no other witnesses it was basically still his word against mine! Even though our detectives found reason to believe he had done this to many other women who had been in his company but had no hard evidence other than their recollections would allow.

The predator invoked the 5th Amendment on every question asked of him during his deposition.

> *The Fifth Amendment to the U.S. Constitution guarantees that an individual cannot be compelled by the government to provide incriminating information about himself—the so-called "right to remain silent." When an individual "takes the Fifth," he invokes that right and refuses to answer questions or provide information that might incriminate him.*

They confiscated his phone, but could never access it without his password and he didn't have to provide it. So they were unable to obtain any further information from him or even prove if he had a prescription or access to the drugs he put in my water that night. Ultimately, the criminal case was dismissed without prejudice, leaving me with lingering questions and a deep sense of injustice. It was soul-crushing.

Yet, being as relentless as I had become, I refused to back down. The battle for justice took a new form as I pressed forward with the civil suit. The courtroom became the arena where truth would finally have its day. I sued not only the rapist but also his team of attorneys separately for defamation of character, relentlessly pursuing the justice that had eluded me for so long. I'm not going to lie, it was a grueling process that nearly killed me and I hesitate to advise anyone else to go this route. It isn't for the faint of heart and I lost 3 pivotal years of my life in my efforts.

Chapter 15: A Battle for Justice

The two female attorneys on his team eventually settled, but as for his arrogant lawyer the cockroach who called the press conference, stubbornly refused to settle, so I took him to trial—it lasted a couple of weeks and the verdict was unequivocal: a unanimous jury decision in my favor. I was so overwhelmed by this conclusion that I don't even recall what the jury said to me, but they were so outraged by my experience and I remember them all kindly yet sadly smiling when the court bailiff read the verdict.

The victory in this civil suit served as a beacon of hope, a testament to the resilience of the human spirit in the face of overwhelming odds. While the scars of the past would never fully heal, I had reclaimed my power and found a measure of closure in a hard-fought battle for justice, for a moment.

After three excruciating years, the relentless battle against the rapist who had caused me immeasurable pain had drained me of my strength. The fight had worn me down to a mere shadow of myself, devoid of the will to persist in a struggle that seemed to have no end. When the drug-inducing rapist presented a settlement, it felt like a bittersweet surrender. In a state of utter exhaustion, too weary to carry on or even to simply be, I accepted it, not just for myself, but for my children. The sum appeared to be substantial enough to secure their educational future, a glimmer of redemption in the midst of my capitulation. Despite the deep-seated regret that I hadn't provided for them as I had wanted during those turbulent years, I took the settlement, telling myself that at least their college expenses would be covered, and they could start afresh, unburdened by the financial struggles that had overshadowed our lives. And if Steve and I sold our house, we would have enough to get the hell out of that cruel town we had so absolutely come to despise.

That narrative would take a sharp turn not long after, shedding light on the murky intricacies and profound injustices that can lurk within the legal system. After a hard-fought victory in a slander case against the attorneys who had callously disseminated false accusations, tarnishing my reputation and career, a new challenge arose. Just when a sense of empowerment began to take root, the landscape shifted dramatically, revealing the unsettling influence of wealth and connections in the judiciary.

The verdict, which should have been a beacon of hope and reparation, and conveniently after all the news outlets announced my victory, it was undermined when the judge, known to be a friend of the opposing lawyers, made a staggering decision. SHE ruled that the attorneys were exempt from paying the restitution the jury had awarded me. HER justification? That the man responsible for my drugging and assault, the affluent rapist, had already paid "enough with his settlement!" Can you believe it? This ruling was a blatant dismissal of the separate offenses committed by the lawyers—their deliberate actions had irrevocably damaged my career and the trauma from their public calumnies persisted, indelibly linked to my name on the internet. Forever.

This twist was a brutal gut punch, not just for the immediate impact it had on me, but for the stark revelation it provided about the legal system I was navigating. I was left shocked and deeply depressed all over again, grappling with the realization that the judicial system, a structure I had believed was founded on principles of fairness and justice, could be so blatantly skewed by corruption and cronyism. The experience transformed my understanding and trust in the legal process. It was a vivid, infuriating demonstration of how influence and affluence can distort the path of justice, leaving the scales unbalanced and the aggrieved without the restitution they are lawfully due.

This chapter serves not only as a personal account of perseverance and disappointment but also as a cautionary tale. It underscores the harsh reality that justice is not always served where powerful individuals sway the scales, and the fight for what is right can be littered with disheartening revelations and unforeseen betrayals. Yet, it also reinforces the importance of resilience, the power of speaking one's truth, and the necessity for systemic change to truly uphold justice for all.

CHAPTER 16:

Behind the Smile

A Solitary Struggle with Silent Screams

In the depths of my despair, I found myself confronting a familiar, haunting ghost: suicide. This battle I had fought and conquered as a teenager, ever since drawing strength from the knowledge that ending my life back then would have robbed me of all the beautiful moments that would lay ahead. That belief, that things would eventually get better, had been my shield against the darkest moments life had thrown my way.

But this time was different. Exhaustion had taken hold for decades of betrayal, and shame. I felt weary to my core. The relentless ugliness of the world seemed inescapable, I didn't want to witness any more evil, and worst of all, I wholeheartedly believed that my children would be better off without me. My will to live had all but evaporated, and I saw no way out of the darkness that enveloped me. I called my attorney, instructing him to draft a new will, bequeathing everything I had to my children and I gave away my most cherished possessions preparing for what I believed to be my inevitable end.

Sitting on my bed, I gathered up all the pills that had been prescribed to me during this torturous period of therapy and despair. I had no trust in humanity and at this point, I couldn't even trust myself. How could I have let this happen? How did I not know what a sick twisted person this man was? After everything I had been through in my life, and all the people I didn't trust but should have, and all the people I should have been able to trust but couldn't, how in the world was I so stupid to not see through this monstrous human? Was this karma for the mistakes I had made in my past? Was it my fault because I was too nice to him? Is it not okay to have any friendship with a man? He was 20 years older than me. At no time was I attracted to or afraid of him and at no time did I feel he could overpower me in any capacity even if he tried. Being in real estate, I have taken many self-defense classes over the years. Of course, never did I consider the possibility of being drugged to the point of unconsciousness. It didn't matter. I blamed myself.

Every victim harbors a burden of self-blame. It's an innate, albeit torturous, facet of human nature to seek a cause for every effect, to assign reason to the unreasonable. We struggle with the notion that calamities might strike arbitrarily, that chaos can reign without warning. It is even more unsettling to acknowledge that certain individuals roam among us harboring such self-centered or malevolent intent that they would inflict pain without provocation. This search for reason in the unreasonable is often a victim's silent, unacknowledged torment.

I found myself wishing I had remained silent, gone straight home that morning, and remained ignorant of that

Chapter 16: Behind the Smile

night's truths. Until the stark revelations of the toxicology and DNA reports emerged, I harbored a sliver of belief in his midnight assurances over the phone. His words had almost convinced me that my memory gaps, my abrupt blackout, and the injuries—a fractured knee, a broken nose—were the indications of some neurological malady, perhaps a brain tumor beginning its insidious journey.

Despair had gripped me, a complete willingness to relinquish my grasp on everyone and everything that tethered me to this existence, even life itself.

I recall the rare moment I was alone on my bed, a solitude seldom felt these days, as Steve's concern for my well-being had grown almost palpable. On the cusp of succumbing to the seductive escape offered by a mix of Valium and Xanax, the ping of my son's text cleaved the silence. His words, "Mama, can you take me to dinner? I love you," accompanied by the image of a kissing face emoji, halted the momentum of my despair. The thought flickered through my mind—I can always do this afterward. Or maybe this is a sign that I'm making a terrible mistake. So, I placed the bottle down, got dressed, and went to pick him up.

The love I have for my son and daughter, is profound, an indescribable bond that kept me grounded in that moment. Ironically he wanted to have dinner at the very place where this recent drama began. A place I had since purposefully avoided. But this time I was safe and we had a wonderful time. I was happy there with him and a new memory was embedded in my mind.

As I drove home, I reflected on the path I was about to embark upon and I knew it was wrong. I suddenly realized that my kids would certainly not be better off without me. That this was my own twisted illusion. A lie I had convinced myself of so confidently. I also now thought about the irreversible impact my actions would have on them, and I suddenly couldn't bear the thought of leaving them with this devastation and confusion. They didn't really even know what I was going through. I always tried to keep it together in front of them. I remember pulling off the road and crying for the longest time, so grateful that he called.

After I got home, I turned to spiritual videos for solace. One video, in particular, triggered a shift in my perspective. Teal Swan, conveyed the idea that suicide was in fact a terminal illness, and if left untreated, it would inevitably lead to certain death and that the treatment was a drastic change and attention to self. That notion struck a chord within me, prompting me to think more about this.

I thought about my son's text message, and how it had postponed my intentions just long enough for me to experience something special that would bring me joy one last time. It was a glimmer of hope, a lifeline in the darkness. I decided that if I were to end my life, I could clearly do it anytime, I was completely in control of that, but why not first fulfill a long-standing dream from my bucket list and see if that made a difference? Why not travel to a faraway place where I could explore things I had only read about? What do I have to lose? Nothing. In my mind, I was already dead.

I need to say here that the echo left by a life lost to suicide is a haunting that reverberates through the hearts of loved ones with a myriad of emotions—confusion, guilt, sorrow, and an unquenchable yearning for answers. If you find yourself in this heart-wrenching aftermath, please know: that it's not your fault. As survivors in the ripple of this tragedy, we often torture ourselves with relentless

Chapter 16: Behind the Smile

"what ifs" and "if onlys," believing we should have seen, known, or done more. Yet, the stark truth we must come to terms with is that the landscape of a suicidal mind is a terrain so complex, so obscured by the shadows of despair and inner turmoil, that it often remains imperceptible to even the most observant and caring among us.

To the world, my smile was a masterful illusion, a facade of strength meticulously constructed to shield the turmoil raging within. Beneath the beaming curve of joy that I projected, there lay a tempest of despair, a cacophony of silent screams that no one seemed to hear, let alone understand. My pain was an enigmatic puzzle that I bore alone, hidden in plain sight, while seemingly in full control.

My actions, inexplicable as they may have seemed, were misinterpreted through lenses of judgment. To onlookers, I was a paradox—the person with the striking smile who, out of nowhere, seemed to act irresponsibly, even selfishly. Little did they know, each decision that appeared impulsive or self-centered was, in truth, a desperate grasp at survival, a lifeline thrown into the tumultuous seas of my inner world. I wasn't living; I was surviving, battling every single day against an invisible force trying to drown me from the inside out.

The complexity of my journey made it an unspeakable secret, an inner narrative that I believed was incomprehensible to others. How could I reveal the depths of my suffering when it was an experience so profoundly personal, so intricately linked with the shadows of trauma that I wished no other soul ever had to endure? I was convinced that articulating my pain would only be possible if the listener had walked a similar path, a burden I would never wish upon even my worst enemy.

The greatest irony lay in my solitude. In my efforts to protect others from my pain, I inadvertently isolated myself, creating an impenetrable barrier between my truth and those who might have, in their way, understood. But I was guided by an inner conviction that my anguish was an enigma, a labyrinth with no exit, a language without a lexicon.

This chapter is a testament to the silent warriors, the bearers of unseen battles, and the individuals who smile through their agony. Your pain is valid, your survival is a testament to an incredible strength, and your story, however solitary it may seem, resonates on frequencies you may not realize. You are not the embodiment of the misunderstandings others project onto you. You are resilience personified, and your every breath is a defiant proclamation of endurance.

And to those who witness behavior they don't understand, know this: each person carries a history hidden behind their eyes. Rather than judgment, offer empathy; rather than dismissal, practice patience. The story they cannot voice might be a narrative of survival you've never had to live, and the bravest thing they do each day might be the very act of living it.

When enveloped in the darkest corners of their minds, our loved ones couldn't see the tapestry of life's possibilities as we wished they would. Their world, clouded by profound psychological pain, prevented them from absorbing the love, hope, and help extended their way. It's crucial to understand that this wasn't a choice made lightly or selfishly, nor a reflection of our shortcomings in their lives. Rather, it was an unbearable silence they believed they were destined to endure alone, despite every echoing cry from those who cherished them.

Chapter 16: Behind the Smile

However, in the midst of this anguishing journey, there's a beacon of proactive love we can hold onto, a strategy born of empathetic understanding and urgent compassion. If you sense someone teetering on the edge of this precipice, rather than trying to argue them back to safety with assurances of life's beauty, consider agreeing—life can be overwhelmingly hard. Validate their feelings without judgment, then gently propose a deferral: "If you're at the end of your rope, let's do something extraordinary first. Let's step away from the ledge and embark on an experience, just for a while."

Consider this approach the emotional equivalent of a "Make-A-Wish" for a soul in crisis. A suicidal person indeed suffers a terminal illness. This isn't about distraction but connection, creating a space for respite from their inner storm. By embarking on a journey—whether it's a physical trip or simply a mental or emotional break from routine—you're offering an invaluable gift: time. Time for emotions to settle, perspectives to shift, and the unforeseen possibility of healing to peek through the clouds.

My own life was saved in this way. When all seemed lost, it was the act of leaving everything behind to embrace a sliver of extraordinary that rewove the frayed threads of my will to live. It's not a guaranteed solution, but a chance—a chance that the person you love might see a horizon of hope they had believed extinguished.

In the aftermath of loss, or in the fight to prevent it, remember this: You are not to blame for the battle waged within the confines of a loved one's mind. Your love is a powerful light, and sometimes, it's the promise of a shared adventure away from the dark that can lead a soul back home. I had always yearned to sail across the Pacific Ocean on a small sailboat, despite my lack of sailing experience and the absence of a boat. With newfound determination, I quit my job and applied online to be a crew member on sailboats, with the full intention of stopping at nothing to accomplish at least that last goal.

Chapter 17:

Sailing Through Stars

A Voyage of Rediscovery

"The moment you commit, the universe conspires to assist you"

—Emmerson

As the sun dipped below the horizon, its final rays surrendered to the twinkle of stars overhead, a transition so subtle yet profound, mirroring my own journey from despair to awakening. There I was, just a month after searching for a crew position, aboard the Inspirity, a 50-foot Lagoon catamaran—my sanctuary and vessel into a new chapter of existence. Captain Oliver, a Swiss maestro of engineering who spoke the lyrical languages of French, English, and German, was our leader and lover of the big old blue. His first mate and partner in both life and adventure was Brenda, a woman whose laughter seemed to dance on the ocean breeze. Completing our crew were Suel, the meticulous German engineer, Koa, a Hawaiian college student whose spirit was as vast as the seas and my now husband, Steve. This remarkable journey would take me to places both within and beyond myself.

Our odyssey commenced in La Paz, Mexico, with a destination as enigmatic as my quest for healing: the Marquesas the largest island group in French Polynesia, nearly 3000 nautical miles in total. Inspirity was a marvel, equipped with not just sails, but a water maker, induction stove, and solar panels. We even had a 3D printer on board—our assurance against the unpredictable tantrums of the sea. When something broke—we would print a new part in the middle of the ocean!

Forty days we were cradled by the ocean, a world measured not in miles traveled but in the transformation of soul. It was a vast canvas of blue, stretching as far as the eye could see, and we were but a tiny speck in the midst of its grandeur. We celebrated the crossing of the equator by salsa dancing on deck, a milestone amidst the infinite blue, feasting on sushi from our catch of the day. The ocean bestowed upon us gifts of companionship—dolphins, sharks, and whales graced our journey, reminding us that even in isolation, we were never truly alone. And as Oliver said, "Land is never far, it's three miles away... straight down!"

Still, the sea does not always whisper; it sometimes howls, as I learned very well enduring Iniki. A storm bore down on us early in our voyage, a tempest wild enough to fracture my ribs but not my spirit, thanks to the unwavering support of my fellow voyagers. A rogue wave tossed us and me directly into the side of the deck. Amid the agony, my emotions swirled like a tempest within me, and my ire was directed squarely at the heavens. I unleashed my pent-up frustrations and bitterness in a torrent of curses, my voice carried away by the winds. I accused God of cruelty, of indifference to my suffering. Of all the suffering in the world, I screamed my grievances at the sky. And I begged to know why!

Yet, as the days turned into weeks, and I found myself enveloped by nothing but water and sky, a profound transformation began to unfold. In the solitude of the open sea, far removed from the distractions and influences of the world I had known, I embarked on a journey of profound self-discovery and spiritual awakening. It was as though the universe itself had responded to my cries, unveiling truths that had long eluded me. Healing came under starlight, in the bioluminescent waters that seemed to merge with the night sky. It was there, suspended between the stars and the sea, that I could no longer discern where the ocean's embrace ended and the universe's began.

Beneath the cerulean expanse of the ocean's surface, we entered a world as alien as any otherworldly atmosphere. All of us were certified divers so we spent many days exploring the water. It was here, in this submerged realm of silent depths and shifting light, that we encountered the gentle giants of the sea—whale sharks. On one particularly heart-stopping occasion, I found myself floating alongside one of these colossal beings, its body dwarfing even the size of our house back home. It was terrifying and magnificent at the same time.

As immense as the whale shark was, there was a serene grace to its movements. Suspended in the vast blue, it drifted effortlessly, this giant amongst the currents, unconcerned with my proximity. Feasting on clouds of krill, it seemed a leviathan set against the delicate ballet of the ocean's smaller inhabitants. I recall the gripping realization that a single, sudden move from the shark could send me tumbling through the water, yet its calm demeanor held steadfast, a testament to the creature's gentle nature. I remember, it looking like it was barely even moving and yet I struggled to keep up with it, swimming as fast as I could—I could not stay with it for very long.

Equally breathtaking was the dance with wild dolphins, creatures of intelligence and curiosity that rivaled the most vivid of dreams. I had once shared the laughter of my children in a controlled encounter with dolphins in a Caribbean pool, but this was different. To be a part of the ocean's pulse, to swim amongst dolphins in their untamed world, was to touch a kind of magic—raw and unfiltered.

These encounters imprinted upon me a profound respect and a sense of unity with the natural world. To be accepted, even for a moment, into the fold of such majestic creatures' lives was to experience a wonder that transcends the ordinary—a remarkable privilege that underscored the vastness and the beauty of our planet's aquatic tapestry.

I came to grasp the enchantment that infuses our world and the purpose that guides our existence. Life, I realized, is a wondrous and intricate tapestry where we bear witness to the full spectrum of human emotion. It is a journey that encompasses the deepest of sorrows and the most radiant of joys.

It is as if consciousness itself asked, "What Am I?" And God answered, producing every single imagined possibility.

We are here to witness everything that exists and to reflect on the marvels and intricacies of being, to explore the vastness of experience, and to add our own unique thread to the intricate web of existence.

Chapter 17: Sailing Through Stars

The initial anger and despair that had consumed me gradually yielded to a newfound sense of serenity and understanding. The pain that I had once resisted and resented now became an essential part of my human experience, a sensation meant to be felt and acknowledged. I was no longer burdened by the weight and regret of my past, but rather, I embraced each moment as a vital piece of the intricate puzzle of life.

Amid the ebb and flow of our nautical odyssey, Steve embarked on a personal voyage of his own—a whimsical challenge to not shave throughout our forty days at sea. As the sun rose and set, his beard grew into a magnificent bristle, each strand weaving tales of the winds and tides we'd encountered, until it became as much a part of him as the sea was now a part of us.

My own transformation was of a different nature, marked not by growth, but by absence. The demands of the sea are unrelenting, and our resources were not immune to its humor. When our water maker faltered, the waves seemed to rise in mocking turmoil, and for a time, I succumbed to the ocean's churn. With dehydration tipping the scales, I grew lighter, my body surrendering its reserves to the sea. Seasickness gripped me, a relentless reminder of our vulnerability even in the face of vast beauty.

In those moments, huddled over the side of the boat or clutching my steadfast companion—a bucket soon christened 'Ralph' by the crew—I found a strange kinship with the water that both sustained and tormented me. The weight of the ocean's vastness was literal and figurative, a burden we all carried until land finally embraced us once again.

It was a profound lesson in humility and survival, a testament to our adaptability. The sea, ever the stern teacher, showed us that life at its most elemental is both taking and giving, a cycle as constant as the tides.

As our vessel nudged closer to the promise of land, the mood aboard was a tapestry of anticipation and silent relief. The intimacy of our shared quarters, once a cocoon, began to fray at the edges. Conversations that had once flowed like the tides now ebbed, as if we'd exhausted not just the sea's stories but our own. We were mariners inching toward the finish line, bound by a complex knot of camaraderie and a mutual yearning for solitude.

The sight of land on the horizon acted as a balm to our weary spirits. We longed not just for the solid earth beneath our feet, but for the simple, expansive joy of personal space—the luxury of anonymity within a crowd, the quiet that comes with distance. Dreams of the shore's embrace, with its sprawling beaches, promised the sweet solace of sand sifting between our toes, a tactile contrast to the unyielding decks that had been our world.

And so, as the first whispers of earth's scent mingled with the salty air, we prepared to part ways, not with grand gestures, but with knowing nods. It was time to unfurl ourselves from the tight ship's company, to stretch into the spaciousness of land, and to rediscover the parts of ourselves left dormant by the demands of the sea.

Our sanctuary emerged on the horizon as the primitive island of Nuku Hiva, a land untouched and unspoiled. The locals, guardians of nature's wisdom, unveiled the harmony of existence, the very inspiration that had moved the director of "Avatar," James Cameron, to breathe life into a world beyond dreams. They, too, breathed life into my shattered world, teaching me the sacred dance of coexistence with the universe.

Chapter 17: Sailing Through Stars

Beneath the waves, I found solace and wonder, diving into realms where few humans dared to roam. Amongst coral kingdoms and aquatic marvels, I discovered not just the will to survive, but an insatiable hunger to thrive. The ocean depths whispered ancient secrets, entreating me to continue my exploration of this magnificent world we are blessed to call home.

As land faded into memory and stars once again became my canopy, I realized that this voyage was more than a sojourn across the sea. It was a pilgrimage to the heart of existence. I fell irrevocably in love with life, with the mysteries cradled in the cosmos, and with the uncharted landscapes within my own soul. The universe, with its infinite wonders, beckoned me to continue this wondrous odyssey, an invitation to a lifelong quest to explore, to experience, to be.

Returning home was a voyage of its own—a journey laced with paradox. I had voyaged across the world, through its waters and cultures, only to find the hardest stretch of sea was the one leading back to the harbor of 'home.' The metamorphosis within me was profound; I was no longer the person who had set sail. I felt estranged amidst familiar settings, a feeling exacerbated by my family's lack of understanding, with the exception of my dad, who understood. They viewed my departure as a whimsical escape, unable to see the despair I had circumnavigated. They couldn't fathom the dark precipice I had tiptoed along before finding salvation in the embrace of the horizon.

Their interpretation of my actions—irresponsible, selfish, perhaps even mad—was a narrative starkly different from my lived reality. They hadn't witnessed the violent tempests of my past, nor the inner turmoil I had weathered. To them, my transformation was an enigma, a radical shift that was as alien as it was unsettling.

I found myself alien in my own land, a stranger to those who shared my blood. The disconnect was palpable; conversations with old friends became like navigating through a foreign dialect. The inability to bridge that gap left me adrift in a place that should have been my anchorage. The feeling of not belonging gnawed at me, a poignant reminder that sometimes, the most arduous part of a journey is not leaving, but returning.

Acceptance became my compass in the uncharted aftermath of my return. It dawned on me that the understanding I sought from others was not a shore I could anchor at but a mirage on the horizon of their perceptions. Thus, I resolved to embrace the odyssey of self-discovery that had so irrevocably altered my being.

Forging a new path required the fortitude of a solitary sailor facing the open sea. I had to become the custodian of my own journey, charting a course through life that was authentic to the person I had blossomed into. No longer could I seek validation in familiar eyes that no longer recognized me; instead, I turned inwards, to the compass of my soul, to navigate the waves of existence.

This internal voyage was not without its storms. There were moments of doubt, of longing for the comfort of shared understanding. Yet, there was also liberation in the realization that my path was mine alone to tread. The person I had become—tempered by trials, broadened by experience, and enriched by an array of cultures—was not bound by the expectations of a past life or the misunderstanding of well-meaning kin.

Chapter 17: Sailing Through Stars

In my reflections on existence, I am drawn to a profound truth: to thrive in this world, we must embrace three vital capabilities. The first is to love with a recognition of life's fleeting nature and to cherish what is transient. The second is to cradle this precious life close to our hearts as if the very rhythm of our pulse depended upon it. And finally, we must muster the courage to release it with grace when the time arrives.

In stepping forward on my own path, I stepped into a world ripe with possibility, a realm where I could live not just in accordance with who I had been, but who I had courageously become.

A Letter to My Son

A note I found while gathering my notes for this book

Cam,

    I'm having such an amazing time out here in the middle of the Pacific Ocean. I have gone through nearly every emotion possible during these past three and a half weeks and I really miss you. I'm now in this wonderful place of acceptance and peace that I have only experienced once before in my life and that is when you were born. I feel completely happy and free of all life's little insecurities. Free from the judgment of others… free from the expectations of others and full of so much love and appreciation for life that I could burst! The world and all its beauty have become so insanely special to me. Special in ways that I can't really describe in words, but I'll try.

Bioluminescence—
    The water at night has to be one of the most spectacular phenomena I have ever witnessed with my own eyes. The water lights up at night like the Milky Way and as the bows of our boat push through

the water it creates just enough chaos for them to light up the sea in their dance... I hope you have the chance to see this someday. It literally brings me to tears it's so perfectly beautiful.

Birds—
You know how when you imagine being lost at sea, day after day, week after week, drifting with no land in sight... floating and waiting for some as-semblance of land to appear on the horizon... and the one thing you imagine would surely appear in front of your eyes, as you stare prayerfully at the blazing sun and sky above, that you would see a majestic bird gracefully floating by on a breeze as an indication that if you looked up that land would finally be within in eyesight... at least that's the way they set it up in any movie or documentary I have ever seen...

It isn't true. Birds are out here in the middle of the ocean, all by themselves. Dead smack in the center of the Pacific Ocean with no land in sight in any direction for at least 1,750 nautical miles anyway... that's 450 hours of sailing at 5.8 knots! So far from land. They rest on the waves and all they seem to do is hunt for fish. At night I think they sleep on our mast because we have found a bit of poop as evidenced on several occasions. Maybe they even started out by following us from the last island we left and simply got lost out here... They keep my mind occupied and I have given them names... there are three of them and seemingly all males, so I call them Meni, Miney, and Joe. Joe is a jerk and always tries to take away from the others or bully them around, but they just keep doing what they do... hunting. Eating. Playing in the water. Every day. All day. No idea where they are going I pretend, but it appears that they are coming with us to French Polynesia nonetheless. Maybe they are migrating there with us... maybe they know exactly what they are doing. Why do I assume that they do not?

As I experience this wonderful world that God has created, I can't help but hope you one day do something like this too. In fact, I'm going to insist that you travel for at least one year before you finish college... if you go to college. My advice to you is this... travel. Learn to race cars. Get a degree in something that interests you... ANYTHING. But it MUST interest you greatly... if it's history... great! 4-year degree in history it is... and oh how I pray you go back to your music someday. But travel. Enjoy the world and your life. Don't ever do a single thing for the money or because it pays well... Cam if you hear anything I have ever said to you please let it be this... your purpose in this life is to live it and to experience it... all of it. You were given skin to feel... feel everything and learn to love and enjoy every emotion. Ears to hear... hear everything. Including pain and loss... because you will have it. We can't prevent it, but we can control how we perceive it and how we choose to accept its presence. Do what your heart tells you to do... no matter what anyone else would say or think about it... you come from a long line of very stubborn, intelligent, risk-taker, competitive, charming, deeply in-tuned, sensitive, kind, and loving people. We are also all very eccentric and different from others... believe this is a gift. Nurture it. Make your own path. Do what your heart tells you in any and all circumstances. Your heart and gut instinct will never fail you if you listen.

You taught me one of the most important lessons I think any of us can ever learn in life... we don't see things are they are, we see things as we are. "The mind is a powerful force. It can enslave us or empower us. It can plunge us into the depths of misery or take us to the heights of ecstasy. Learn to use the power wisely."—David Cuschieri

I've often heard, that more than anything sons need their moms to love and accept them for who they are. I hope that my love and acceptance have always been apparent to you, though I wish I could have had the opportunity more in the last couple of years.

You are a remarkable person and I see you as an evolution of us... so there is no doubt in my mind that you will succeed in whatever you set out to achieve in life, because when we fail... we fail forward!

Here are a few tidbits I'll leave you with:

- Telling the truth is a great strength, it can be hard, but ultimately it's what separates the men from the boys. Telling the truth can be really hard sometimes, but it is the right thing to do, always
- Communicate with those you love. It's important to our growth and for those close to you to know what you are thinking, and feeling. Also, when we don't communicate we tend to make assumptions about situations and most often

Chapter 17: Sailing Through Stars

those assumptions are completely inaccurate! So use your voice!
- Be patient with people, especially your little sister. She looks up to you so help and protect her always.
- You know this by now, but bullies will always be around. You can't control them or allow them to get under your skin. You can only control what you do and my best advice is simply to avoid them and walk away whenever possible. Believe me, it's hard. Turning the other cheek does not come easy for me either, but I promise you in the end it's in your own best interest. Forgiveness is a major key to happiness in this life.
- Relax and don't sweat the small stuff. Not something I excel in but as time goes on, I worry less about things I cannot control. My sense tells me you'll master this attribute easier than me.
- Educate yourself and never stop learning. Find something you enjoy doing and put your heart and soul into it and It will never seem like work.
- Manage your resources responsibly. Save money so that when times are tough or you need to help someone else you can. Yet, don't be afraid to splurge on yourself either.
- Never be afraid to ask out the best-looking girl in the room!

Cam, you are a born leader. You inspire without even trying. Stay true to yourself and don't let anyone or anything define you. Only you get to do that.

I love you guys more than anything, I thank God for you and your sister every single day. I am so proud of you both and it is an honor to be your mom. I'm looking forward to sharing in your life's journey and all the special moments yet to come.

—Mama

CHAPTER 18:

The Observer and the Observed

My thirst for knowledge had grown insatiable during my time at sea. I delved into the teachings of various religions, and spiritual guides, explored the mysteries of quantum physics, and contemplated ancient civilizations like the Anunnaki. I nurtured my connection to the Earth through gardening and gazed upon the stars, finding solace in the cosmos through both astronomy and astrology.

In order for the sun to be acknowledged as the sun, it must be perceived as such. This is not just poetic musing; it mirrors a principle of quantum physics, where observation influences the state of the observed. This interplay of perception and reality is as fundamental as the age-old riddle of the chicken and the egg, which, in its magical conundrum, suggests that both must arise simultaneously.

Consider the monumental instances of creation—the Big Bang, the formation of galaxies, cellular division, the moment of conception—where the observer and the observed seem to merge into a singular event. This essence of consciousness echoes through my musings; it's the heart of our being, a singularity at the core of existence.

My influence, my financial status, and my very essence are recognized only if perceived by others and believed by myself. Just as a tree's fall in a deserted forest remains silent, our existence hinges on this duality of perception. From conception, our beliefs shape us, the energy of our thoughts weaving into the fabric of our reality.

The law of attraction and the concept of a mirror universe touch upon this, but the fabric of existence is richer still. Belief in oneself is reciprocal—if I falter in self-belief, I cannot expect others to believe in me. Similarly, if I lose faith in another, it can lead to a cascading loss of their own self-belief. The genesis of this cycle is immaterial; what matters is its resolution.

I propose that confidence is the currency of reality, accounting for half of what defines us. The other half is validation through another's belief in us. Confidence alone is insufficient; if we tarnish our image, we are undone, trapped in the cacophony of noise and false perceptions that plague society today.

Understanding the full narrative of a person's life would undoubtedly foster empathy, comprehension, and compassion. Life, I believe, is waiting to reveal such understanding, the promise of ultimate peace and knowledge, and the realization that our shared struggles stem from this simple lack of understanding. Perception is the artisan of our reality.

Perhaps we are too far gone, perhaps not all are meant to believe in this interconnectedness. Yet, my realization remains clear—how do we manifest this? We rebuild, step by step, acknowledging beauty, embracing flaws, and appreciating differences. It's about seeing the gift in what

Chapter 18: The Observer and the Observed

might otherwise irritate, understanding those we disagree with, and valuing their stories.

We must be willing to share our narratives, the good and the bad, to allow others to learn from our journey. We falter, we err, but we also rise, learn, and shine. As we continue to search, we find; as we aim to see, we understand. The more expansive our view, the clearer we see that every perspective has its truth and fallacy.

Realizing our profound interconnectedness is key. To harm another is to harm oneself—it is a law of nature. In this last chapter of reflections, I urge a shift in perception, to embrace the totality of life, and in doing so, find the balance that allows us to see, to believe, and ultimately, to exist in harmony.

I'd like to share a perspective that I believe could illuminate our shared journey. I hold a conviction, one that resonates deeply within me, that all of existence is intertwined—energetically fused at a fundamental level. This connection transcends our individual notions of the divine, whether we frame it as God, the Universe, Allah, or the principles of Quantum Physics. We are, in essence, a singular entity experiencing itself through an infinite array of perspectives.

To bring this concept to life, imagine each of us as a unique snowflake. Originating from the same source—mere droplets in the vast atmosphere—every snowflake embarks on its own path. As they drift through space and time, these droplets crystallize into forms of intricate beauty, each distinct in shape, size, and hue. To the casual observer, each flake seems entirely separate from the rest, yet at their core, they are identical, composed of the same water that remembers its journey.

This metaphor is the heart of a children's book I'm also writing, "Luna the Snowflake's Song", aiming to convey that despite the apparent differences forged by our individual experiences, we are fundamentally the same, and eventually, we all return to that shared essence. The notion that water has memory serves as a poignant reminder that our actions ripple through time, carrying the essence of our deeds far beyond our immediate perception.

Understanding our oneness might seem esoteric, but it carries a profound implication: every act of kindness, every gesture of empathy, every moment of patience, is a thread woven into the fabric of humanity's evolution. Such change is gradual, often surpassing our lifetimes, yet the faith in this slow transformation is what sustains the hope for a better future.

As we navigate this existence, I hold onto the belief that our self-perception is a powerful architect of our reality. The image we cultivate of ourselves—our self-concept—is the mold from which our lives take shape. Recognizing this, and seeing others as extensions of ourselves, we unlock the potential to be anything we choose. It's in this understanding and the recognition of our collective identity that the seemingly nonsensical aspects of life become clearer, and the true nature of our interconnectedness becomes undeniable. The changes we inspire today may not bear immediate fruit, but with patience and steadfastness, we contribute to the ever-unfolding evolution of consciousness, shaping not just our own destiny, but that of the entire cosmos

At first through modern therapy, I was repeatedly told that I bore the weight of a disorder. The recent trauma had bestowed upon me the mantle of post-traumatic stress disorder (PTSD) and anxiety, and the accumulated traumas of

Chapter 18: The Observer and the Observed

my life, from the hurricane to the domestic violence of my childhood, and the tragic murder of my uncle were seen as evidence of chronic complex post-traumatic stress disorder (C-PTSD) a disorder that had no known cure. Are you kidding me? I had been branded with a label of mental illness, permanent damage, forever defined by the malice and mistakes of others. This notion was unacceptable and did not align with my belief system. It seemed illogical and inconceivable that the actions of others could fundamentally break me or define my worth. I rejected the idea of being forever damaged or unwell due to circumstances beyond my control. I refused to be confined by labels that reduced me to the sum of my traumas. It was during my time at sea, amid the boundless expanse of the ocean, that I resolved to reshape my perspective.

In the exploration of self and consciousness, the words "I think, therefore I am" take on a transformative power. This statement isn't just an affirmation of existence; it's a testament to the human condition, reflecting our ability to shape our own identity through thought. What we conceive within the intricacies of our mind often manifests in the reality of our lives. Our thoughts about ourselves don't just define us—they set the boundaries of our potential. If we believe we are capable, resilient, or innovative, we embody these qualities, creating a self-fulfilling prophecy energized by our own cognition. This isn't merely existence; it's conscious creation, a continual process of becoming, fueled by the very act of thought itself. So, when we say, "I think, therefore I am," we're also declaring, "As I think about myself, so shall I become," acknowledging thought as the powerful sculptor of our ever-evolving identity.

In the midst of what felt like my darkest hour, I underwent a profound transformation of thought. I realized that I was more than the sum of my experiences and that my identity extended far beyond the traumas I had endured. Labels did not define me, and I would not accept their limitations. Instead of being a victim, I chose to embrace the concept of "post-traumatic growth."

I recognized that the adversities I had faced had endowed me with unique strengths. My heightened awareness of my surroundings, and my ability to consider multiple outcomes and be prepared for any situation—these were indeed qualities that would now set me apart. They were no longer weaknesses but rather powerful assets.

Through every challenge and triumph, I have clung to a simple yet profound mantra: "I think, therefore I am." These words, a beacon of enlightenment philosophy, have been my anchor, reminding me that my existence is affirmed through my thoughts and my consciousness. It is a testament to the power of the mind, a power that has propelled me across oceans and continents, through joy and sorrow, and into the quiet reflection of Montana's starlit nights. Where I now call home.

This mantra has guided me to understand that my reality is crafted by perception, and shaped by the vigor of my thoughts. It's a call to live deliberately, to engage with the world in full consciousness, to be present in every moment. As I continue to weave the tapestry of my life, these words resonate within me, fueling my conviction that awareness is the essence of my being, the core from which I draw strength to face the infinite possibilities of tomorrow.

Through this journey, I discovered that our beliefs shape our reality. I am what I believe I am. I realized that

Chapter 18: The Observer and the Observed

I possessed the power to heal and become stronger. I nurtured a heightened empathy, compassion, and capacity for love and forgiveness that surpassed anything I had known before. I understood that purpose, effort, and action were the keys to achieving my goals and that my beliefs had the power to manifest my reality.

This realization was the cornerstone of my transformation. I had emerged from the depths of despair not as a broken individual but as a resilient and empowered soul. I had chosen to grow from my traumas rather than be defined by, or ashamed of them, and in doing so, I had unlocked the immense potential within myself.

Do I still have bad days?

Yes, the bad days still visit, as inevitable as a shadow in a world with light. Healing isn't a linear journey, nor a destination with a clear path etched before me. It's a winding road that traverses landscapes of my psyche I'm still learning to understand, with uphill battles that test the very sinews of my soul. But now, there's a fundamental difference in my visit through these peaks and valleys: I bear the wisdom that nothing is permanent, and everything, whether joy or pain, demands its moment in the sun. And I give myself permission to just stay in bed all day and cry when I need to, or take the day off from work and go play with my dog and explore nature.

This isn't about negating the hardships or glorifying the struggles. It's about acknowledging that life, in all its tumultuous beauty, is a mosaic of transient states. Just as the highest moments of elation gently ebb away into the tides of memory, so too does the deepest pain eventually recede, leaving behind echoes that resonate with the enduring strength of our spirit.

Now, when the dark days drape their heaviness around me, I permit myself to feel—to truly feel it. I let the pain cascade through every vein, every sinew, every fragment of my being because I know it's a testament to my humanity, a poignant reminder of my capacity to endure and emerge, time and time again. These moments of despair are no longer suffocating dead-ends; they are profound teachers, stark reminders of my own resilience, and a precursor of brighter days that will come.

Moreover, this journey has taught me an invaluable lesson: every emotion is a guest, some unwelcome, some dearly cherished, but none a permanent resident. I've learned to sit with my feelings, to offer them the acknowledgment they demand, and then, in time, to let them go. This ebb and flow is no easy tide to navigate, but it's a natural rhythm I've learned to respect. It's an ongoing conversation with my soul, a delicate dance between despair and hope, and the very pulse of my continued healing.

To those treading their paths: remember, you're not alone in the undulating journey of recovery. Your bad days, those uphill battles, are just a part of the larger narrative of your resilience. They're proof that you're moving, feeling, and most importantly, living. Keep going, for the road ahead promises vistas of hope, strength, and renewed joy.

Remember, just as the pain demands to be felt, it also demands to be released, giving way to new dawns, new joys, and the perpetual rhythm of your beautiful, beating heart. In the grand tapestry of life, I now tread fearlessly, fully aware that death is an inevitable part of our journey. Each moment is a cherished gift, and even the capacity to feel pain is a reminder that we are alive and experiencing the richness of existence. The uncertainty of when our

Chapter 18: The Observer and the Observed

time will come lingers, but it serves as a poignant reminder to live every moment to the fullest.

In the tapestry of our lives, the past is not a fixed canvas but a dynamic backdrop that can be reinterpreted and transformed by the future. Much like a complex melody, the true essence of our experiences often remains elusive until the later notes fall into place, each one shedding new light on the ones that came before it. As we journey through time, it's the unfolding of life's events that gradually reveals a clearer, more complete picture. With each new experience, we are given the chance to understand our past not as an immutable truth, but as a part of a larger, ever-evolving narrative, where meaning is derived not solely from a single moment but from the symphony of all that follows.

No longer do I squander my precious seconds fretting over yesterday, for the past is an unchangeable landscape. Time, like a flowing river, moves inexorably forward, and while we can dip our hand into its current, we can never touch the same water again.

I have learned that, while I cannot control the actions of others, I hold the reins of my own destiny firmly in my grasp. I have shed the weight of labels and embraced the power of self-belief, turning adversity into an opportunity for growth.

The pages of my passport are now emblazoned with the stamps of fifty-two countries, each a chapter in the grand adventure that has been my life. From the deep azure mysteries of Belize's Great Blue Hole to the serene majesty of Switzerland's Glacier Express, I've sought the pulse of the world in every corner. I've marveled at the hushed reverence within the walls of the Vatican, felt the whispers of history in the House of the Virgin Mary in Ephesus, and embraced the liberating haze of Amsterdam's cafes. Under the glow of the Eiffel Tower, champagne in hand, life seemed to pause in its beauty.

Each high-speed journey from Belgium to Barcelona was a thread weaving the rich tapestry of my narrative. In these endless moments, I learned the goodness of strangers, the kindness of new friends, and the shared humanity that binds us all.

Now, nestled in the rugged embrace of Bigfork, Montana, my life continues to unfurl in quiet splendor. The night sky here is a canvas of celestial wonder, often streaked with the ethereal dance of the Aurora Borealis. It's a reminder of the universe's vast beauty—a beauty echoed in the dreams of my children, whom I support with the fierce passion of a mother whose love knows no bounds.

As the world grappled with the uncertainty of a pandemic, I watched with a tranquil heart, certain in the belief that all would be well in the end. This conviction guides me through life's turbulence, a sturdy helm as I navigate the seas of the unknown. I've embraced existence with a resounding 'yes,' and treat each soul with a reverence born from a life rich with varied tapestries. I stand ready for the next chapter, eyes wide with wonder, heart open to the infinite possibilities that beckon.

As I conclude this chapter of my life, after having looked back at it now so thoroughly in writing it all down and crying my eyes out each step of the way. I do so with a heart brimming with gratitude. I march boldly into the future, unburdened by fear, and inspired by the endless possibilities that lie ahead. Life is a gift, and I intend to unwrap it fully, savoring each moment, and living with purpose, passion, and an unshakable belief in the limitless potential of the human spirit.

Chapter 18: The Observer and the Observed

With these reflections, I bid farewell to this book, with the hope that my journey may inspire others to navigate their own paths with courage, resilience, and the unwavering determination to embrace life in all its splendor. Stay curious, be on purpose and when you fall, fall forward!

Informational Chapters Follow

CHAPTER 19:

Lingering Shadows

Understanding PTSD

Post-Traumatic Stress Disorder (PTSD) is a complex mental health condition triggered by experiencing or witnessing a terrifying event. Dr. Chivonna Childs, a staff psychologist at the Cleveland Clinic, emphasizes that PTSD is clinically recognized as a response to trauma, often manifesting through flashbacks, nightmares, severe anxiety, and uncontrollable thoughts about the event.

The U.S. National Institute of Mental Health (NIMH) highlights that PTSD can arise from various situations, such as directly experiencing a traumatic event, witnessing trauma inflicted upon others, or learning about violent or unexpected traumatic events.

In certain cases, individuals may develop complex PTSD (C-PTSD), a form of PTSD resulting from enduring trauma over an extended period. According to the CPTSD Foundation, this type of PTSD typically stems from repeated, prolonged traumatic events, often involving a breach of trust or safety, particularly during formative years. Robyn

E. Brickel, director and lead therapist at Brickel and Associates, distinguishes C-PTSD from traditional PTSD by the prolonged, relationship-based trauma that deeply affects the nervous system and attachment relationships.

PTSD symptoms can be pervasive, affecting all aspects of life. The NIMH outlines criteria for diagnosing PTSD, which include experiencing distressing symptoms for more than a month, severe enough to disrupt daily activities and relationships. These symptoms encompass re-experiencing trauma through nightmares or flashbacks, avoidance of trauma-related stimuli, negative changes in thoughts or mood and heightened reactivity.

PTSD doesn't have a single cause but can be precipitated by various traumatic experiences, such as personal or witnessed injuries, life-threatening events, childhood trauma, or additional stress post-trauma. Factors contributing to the risk of developing PTSD include past mental health issues, lack of support, additional post-traumatic stress, or a history of substance abuse. Furthermore, racial trauma is identified as a significant risk factor for PTSD by the National Center for PTSD.

Treating PTSD involves a combination of psychotherapy and often medication. Psychiatry.org recommends several forms of cognitive behavioral therapy (CBT), including cognitive processing therapy, trauma-focused CBT for younger populations, eye movement desensitization and reprocessing (EMDR), and prolonged exposure therapy. Medications, particularly SSRIs and SNRIs, are also common in PTSD treatment. Additionally, alternative therapies and support systems, like service dogs or breathing techniques, have proven beneficial for some individuals.

Chapter 19: Lingering Shadows

PTSD is multifaceted, requiring a holistic approach to therapy. As Dr. Childs articulates, comprehensive support and treatment are crucial for those grappling with PTSD, because everyone deserves a life characterized by quality and wellness.

Choosing a service dog and a holistic approach to managing PTSD is a decision that resonates with many individuals seeking a more integrative method of healing that aligns with their personal preferences, lifestyle, and specific needs. This was the direction that worked best for me.

In the tumultuous wake of my experiences, I found solace in an unexpected ally—a service dog named Dembè. Brought into my life through the suggestion of a victim advocate, and father, this King Poodle, with his obsidian fur, became my anchor. His name was inspired by the loyal guardian Dembè Zuma from "The Blacklist," and was also a serendipitous nod to the African word for peace—a peace I was ardently seeking. As a puppy of only eight weeks, Dembè grew to not only provide companionship but also to assure my safety. He was my steadfast brace, aiding me to stand when I found myself grappling with the weight of my experiences. With his imposing presence, he was a comforting shield, intuitively clearing spaces to grant me a breath of serenity in crowded rooms.

Training Dembè was as much about my growth as it was about his; we learned together, under the guidance of expert trainers, shaping him into an extension of my will, and my needs manifest through his actions. After eight years, Dembè's journey recently took a noble turn—now he extends his service, love, and protection to a neighbor battling ALS, exemplifying the profound impact these creatures have on our lives.

Now, Anunnaki—'Anu' for short—a Belgian Malinois with a spirited intelligence, has stepped into the role once filled by Dembè. Anu is a search-and-rescue marvel, attuned to my every need, capable of retrieving anything I require, and skilled in securing my surroundings. This new bond with Anu is burgeoning, as he's been trained to be attuned to my emotional landscape, providing a waking nudge from the throes of nightmares, and ensuring I am never truly alone. He has also been scent-trained and can smell anything I want him to notice and immediately alert me.

The journey with my service dogs is one of mutual transformation—they, an unwavering presence, and I, a testament to the healing power of their companionship. Anu requires a lot of exercise and he makes sure I get outside every day and keeps me from working too much. I would tell you that he gets me up every day, but that dog would lay in bed for days if I chose to stay there. It's remarkable the level of understanding and acceptance he has for my needs. When a dog is with you 24 hours a day every day they become a part of your very soul. We give each other purpose.

Service dogs are not just pets; they are trained to perform specific tasks that can help alleviate some of the symptoms of PTSD. For instance, they can be trained to recognize signs of anxiety or panic attacks and take action to mitigate them, such as providing a calming presence, creating physical space around the owner in public areas, or even fetching items when you need something out of reach. Their constant companionship offers a sense of security, alleviates feelings of loneliness, and helps re-establish a routine.

Holistic approaches to health, meanwhile, consider the entire person—body, mind, spirit, and emotions—in the quest for optimal health and wellness. In the context of PTSD, this might involve:

1. **Mindfulness and Meditation:** Practices that help ground an individual, bringing attention to the present moment and away from intrusive or distressing thoughts.
2. **Yoga or Tai Chi:** These involve physical postures and breathing techniques that can enhance physical strength, flexibility, and mental clarity, promoting a sense of peace.
3. **Acupuncture or Massage Therapy:** These can help in reducing physical tension and stress, potentially reducing the intensity of PTSD symptoms.
4. **Herbal Supplements or Essential Oils:** Some individuals find these beneficial, but they should be used under the guidance of a healthcare provider, especially considering potential interactions with other medications.
5. **Nutrition and Exercise:** A balanced diet and regular physical activity can improve overall well-being and resilience.
6. **Art or Music Therapy:** Creative expressions can be a non-verbal outlet for emotions and promote healing.
7. **Community or Spiritual Support:** Engaging in group activities or spiritual practices can create a sense of belonging and support.

Complex PTSD (C-PTSD) A psychological disorder (THAT IS CURABLE) can develop in response to prolonged, repeated experiences of interpersonal trauma in a context where the individual has little or no chance of escape. C-PTSD relates to the trauma model of mental disorders and is associated with chronic sexual, psychological, and physical abuse or neglect, chronic intimate partner violence, victims of prolonged workplace or school bullying, victims of kidnapping and hostage situations, indentured servants, victims of slavery and human trafficking, those subjected to genocide campaigns, survivors of concentration camps, and defectors of cults or cult-like organizations. Situations of ongoing abuse, especially if the abuse is perpetrated by someone close to the individual, can interfere with the person's ability to form a secure attachment style and a strong sense of coherent self, which is necessary for mental health.

C-PTSD is characterized by additional symptoms beyond those generally associated with PTSD, including:

1. **Difficulty Regulating Emotions:** This may involve experiencing persistent sadness, extreme exhaustion, suicidal thoughts, explosive anger, or inhibited anger.
2. **Distrust and Alienation:** The individual may feel disconnected from the world or people, not trusting others and feeling alienated from themselves and their emotions.
3. **Emptiness and Hopelessness:** Chronic feelings of emptiness or hopelessness may pervade daily experiences.
4. **Feeling Permanently Damaged:** Individuals may feel they are fundamentally broken or damaged beyond repair.
5. **Difficulty with Relationships:** They may avoid relationships or have trouble sustaining them. They may also be drawn to relationships with dynamics that replicate the abuse they have known.
6. **Dissociation:** Persistent dissociative episodes, during which they feel detached from their emotions or body, are common. This can also manifest as depersonalization or derealization.
7. **Physical Symptoms:** Somatic complaints, especially pain and discomfort without a clear physical origin, are common.

Chapter 19: Lingering Shadows

The symptoms of C-PTSD represent the psychological ramifications of a series of traumatic events that have created a pattern in a person's life, often making it very difficult for the individual to recognize their state as abnormal, further entrenching their symptoms.

Treatment for C-PTSD often involves a multi-faceted approach, typically requiring more long-term and intensive psychotherapy compared to PTSD. This may involve trauma-focused therapy modalities, including but not limited to, cognitive-behavioral therapy (CBT), dialectical behavior therapy (DBT), eye movement desensitization and reprocessing (EMDR), and somatic therapies. Medication may also be prescribed for co-occurring conditions like depression or anxiety. Additionally, support for associated symptoms or conditions, community or family support, education, and lifestyle changes are also crucial in the healing journey.

It's important to work closely with a healthcare professional you trust to determine the most appropriate and effective holistic treatments for you. They can help tailor these practices to your individual needs, ensuring they complement any ongoing traditional treatments and support your journey toward healing and improved quality of life. Remember, the path to managing PTSD is very personal, and what works for one individual may not work for another. It's about finding a balance that suits you personally. BUT, under no circumstances to you ever let anyone tell you that you are broken and that you can not recover from trauma. YES YOU CAN! YOU ARE A SURVIVOR AND YOUR BODY AND MIND WERE BUILT TO HEAL. Period.

CHAPTER 20:

The Hidden Scars

Understanding Sexual Assault

Sexual assault, a term that encompasses a spectrum of unwanted sexual interactions, is a profound violation that unequivocally remains never the victim's fault. Regardless of age or gender, victims often wrestle with self-blame, a heavy burden that compounds their trauma.

Sexual assault involves any type of sexual activity or contact that happens without the explicit consent of the recipient. Forms of sexual assault range from attempted rape to unwanted sexual touching, coercion into performing sexual acts, and rape, which involves the penetration of the victim's body without consent.

Rape, while a form of sexual assault, holds a specific distinction. It's defined legally as sexual penetration without consent, including any slight penetration of the vagina or anus with any body part or object, or oral penetration by a sex organ of another person. Legal definitions of rape vary by state, and for precise state-specific information, it's advised to consult a legal professional or refer to a reliable State Law Database.

The concept of "force" in the context of sexual assault extends beyond physical coercion. Emotional or psychological manipulation, threats against the victim or their loved ones, and other forms of intimidation are all strategies perpetrators use to exert control.

In the majority of cases, the perpetrator is not a masked stranger but someone the victim knows. Data indicates that about eight out of ten sexual assaults are committed by acquaintances, highlighting the prevalence of intimate partner sexual violence and acquaintance rape. The term "date rape" often refers to acquaintance rape, underscoring that prior personal interaction or any level of past intimacy does not imply consent.

Stranger rape, while less common, also manifests in various forms, including blitz sexual assault, contact sexual assault and home invasion sexual assault. Regardless of the perpetrator's identity, survivors often grapple with undue self-blame, internalizing misplaced responsibility for the perpetrator's actions.

It's imperative to reiterate that the victim is never at fault for a perpetrator's heinous actions. Support is available, and speaking with a trained professional can provide much-needed help and guidance. For those seeking assistance, contacting a dedicated Sexual Assault Hotline or engaging in a confidential online chat with a trained professional can offer support and resources.

CHAPTER 21:

Recognizing the Unspoken

Warning Signs in College-Age Adults

The bustling nature of college life is a blend of academic pressures, evolving friendships, and the pursuit of independence. Yet beneath this vibrant atmosphere, there lurks a darker side of the college experience that too often goes unnoticed—sexual assault and abusive relationships. For those surrounding college-age adults—whether you're a parent, professor, friend, or otherwise—understanding the warning signs of such experiences is crucial. Your vigilance and action can potentially change, or even save, a life.

Sexual assault, a horrendous violation, isn't confined by the walls of our homes; it penetrates the seemingly safe boundaries of college campuses and social venues frequented by students. Complicating matters further, in a staggering eight out of 10 cases, the perpetrator is no stranger but someone the victim knows. This uncomfortable truth often shrouds sexual assault in silence, especially if the assailant is a popular student or a supposed 'friend'. Regardless of the perpetrator's identity, survivors shoulder an immense burden and need unwavering support and understanding.

The aftermath of sexual assault is rarely overt, often manifesting in subtle behavioral or physical changes. These signs might be mistakenly attributed to the typical stress of college life, like adapting to a new environment. However, a deeper, more sinister root could be at play. If you spot signs of depression, unexpected withdrawals from activities, unexplained fear, academic decline, or increased substance use, it's imperative to gently reach out. Your approach could be specific, or it might simply offer an open, judgment-free space for disclosure.

Moreover, the specter of sexual assault isn't the only concern. Many college-age adults find themselves entangled in abusive relationships, a context where sexual assault can be a grim reality. Warning signs, such as social withdrawal dictated by the partner, relinquishment of autonomy, or physical injuries, must set off alarm bells. Even more insidious are attempts by an abusive partner to control contraceptive use or pressure into unwanted sexual practices, stripping away bodily autonomy and safety.

In this digital era, abuse extends into the virtual realm. Harassment and violation of consent occur through unsolicited messages, inappropriate sharing of private images, or manipulation using digital platforms. These acts of digital violence create an environment of fear and discomfort, a stark contrast to the freedom and safety that technology promises. Awareness of cyber laws, though varied and complex, is essential in combating this form of abuse.

Your role in noticing these signs cannot be overstated. You are an ally in the shadows, a beacon of hope for those silently suffering. If you suspect someone is a victim of sexual abuse or assault, remember that trained professionals are available to help. Contact the National Sexual Assault Hotline at 800.656.HOPE (4673) or engage in a confidential chat at online.rainn.org. In this fight against sexual violence, your awareness and action are the first steps toward healing and justice.

CHAPTER 22:

Silent Whispers

Warning Signs in Young Children

In the heart of an idyllic childhood, where innocence should thrive, there lurks a sinister reality—every nine minutes, the tranquility is shattered as authorities uncover another instance of child sexual abuse. This abuse transcends the physical act, encompassing exposure to indecency, inappropriate imagery, or even the chilling capture of a child's image in lewd contexts. The repercussions on a young soul are profound, casting long, dark shadows that follow them into adulthood. Recognizing the signs of such abuse is often the first beacon of hope in shielding a child from this devastating storm.

The clandestine nature of sexual abuse makes detection particularly challenging. Perpetrators craft an environment of secrecy and intimidation. However, certain signs are undeniable cries for help, visible to an observant parent, guardian, or caregiver. Trust your instincts. A hint of discomfort, an inexplicable gut feeling around someone in the child's life, merits attention and action. Open the channels of communication with the child, providing a safe harbor for their fears and experiences, articulated in words they understand.

The warning signs manifest across physical, behavioral, and emotional domains. Physical signs such as trauma to intimate areas or sexually transmitted infections scream for immediate medical intervention. Behavioral shifts may include an unusual preoccupation with sexual matters, an uncharacteristic silence, or a reluctance to part with primary caregivers. Witnessing a regression into previously outgrown behaviors like bedwetting or observing abnormal sexual behavior should set off alarm bells. Emotionally, look for changes in eating habits, unexplained fearfulness, or a sudden dip in enthusiasm for school or social activities.

The signals can be complex and, at times, seemingly contradictory—an overly compliant child or one that exhibits oppositional behavior, for instance. The key is a vigilant eye on abrupt behavioral changes. Trust your intuition; do not dismiss it. When a child expresses unease around an individual, even if they cannot pinpoint the reason, your attentive ear is crucial.

Alas, the individuals who inflict such harm often lurk within the circle of trust—a staggering 93 percent of child sexual predators are familiar to their victims. These could be relatives, faith community leaders, coaches, or teachers. Warning behaviors in adults include a disregard for personal boundaries, inappropriate touching, seeking undue time alone with a child, or an unnatural interest in a child's sexual maturation. Be wary of adults who offer unsolicited gifts or attempt to isolate the child from other adults.

Confronting the possibility of abuse is a daunting prospect. The journey towards safeguarding a child may demand significant upheaval in your life. Yet, as echoed by Lisa, a mother and survivor advocate, the guilt and turmoil, though overwhelming, are surmounted by the fierce determination to protect her child. If your instincts signal a threat, delve deeper. Consult with professionals who can guide your next steps and avoid situations that might compromise the child's safety.

You are a silent guardian, and your vigilance is a powerful weapon. If you suspect abuse, do not shoulder this burden alone. Reach out to the National Sexual Assault Hotline at 800.656.HOPE (4673) or seek counsel through a confidential online chat at online.rainn.org. In the realm of a child's whispered fears, your proactive stance can usher in the light of safety and recovery.

CHAPTER 23:

Understanding the Silence in Suffering

I can not stress this point enough; The silent battle against the tempests of the mind is one few can truly comprehend. Despite the grim reality that countless individuals succumb to suicide each year, the recent surge in tragedies among the celebrated has brought to light a truth long articulated by those wrestling with these inner demons: prosperity, stature, professional success, and familial bonds offer no shield against the advance of mental afflictions. Mental illness wages a relentless campaign, often beyond the realm of personal or even professional intervention.

The shockwaves of high-profile suicides ripple through social media, sparking a surge of appeals from newfound mental health champions. Their well-intentioned pleas for open dialogue and assurance of open ears and hearts fail to grasp the complex web of reasons that lead many to suffer in silence. It is a struggle so profound that understanding it is the first step toward prevention.

1. The Stigma of Struggle

Adult life comes with expectations of self-sufficiency—managing basic necessities such as self-care and domestic responsibilities. Mental illness can erode these abilities, leaving individuals feeling demeaned and ashamed. Admitting these struggles can be as daunting as the illness itself, breeding a silence that is often preferred to the discomfort of exposure.

2. The Weight of Burdens

Those grappling with mental health issues may avoid seeking help to not impose on others. They fear confirmation of their inner narrative that they are unworthy of care or that their problems are inconveniences to others. This isolation is a protective measure to shield both themselves and those they care about from the perceived weight of their troubles.

3. The Dread of Dismissal

The act of reaching out is entwined with the risk of rejection or misunderstanding. Vulnerability is a daunting threshold to cross, particularly when there's a chance of being deemed too difficult or being abandoned. For those already in the clutches of mental illness, such a breach of trust can deepen the chasm of isolation and deter future attempts to connect.

4. The Fear of Being Fixed

In seeking an ear to listen, the last thing individuals want is an unsolicited solution. When empathy is substituted with superficial fixes, it invalidates the gravity of their pain and can lead to further withdrawal.

5. The Hurdles to Professional Aid

Navigating the health system for mental support can be a labyrinthine endeavor, often fraught with delays and dismissive interactions. The urgency of mental distress is seldom matched by the availability of immediate and appropriate care, making the exhortation to 'seek help' seem hollow to those in need.

What can society do to extend a lifeline to those in the depths of despair? It is imperative to engage with those around us, to recognize the profound strength it takes to simply appear 'fine,' and to value our loved ones not only in their struggles but also in their everyday existence.

If you know someone who is enduring such a trial, remember that small acts of kindness can have an immeasurable impact. A home-cooked meal, an offer to babysit, an invitation to spend time together, a funny meme, or just a simple message can all be lifelines to someone who feels adrift. Taking the time to understand their condition, to initiate conversations about mental health, or to simply be present can all be powerful interventions.

This chapter not only implores society to be vigilant but also compassionate. By fostering an environment where the dialogue about mental health is open and free from judgment, there can be hope for those who feel their voices are lost in the darkness.

Note to Survivors of Sexual Assault

Navigating the aftermath of sexual assault, especially when it's a trauma endured multiple times, presents a harrowing dilemma. The impulse to remain silent is often fueled by a misguided protection instinct; we convince ourselves we're shielding our loved ones from the corrosive pain of the truth. However, this silence doesn't prevent suffering; it merely cloaks it in confusion, as those around us grapple with our unspoken agony without understanding its source. Conversely, breaking this silence ushers in its own storm of challenges: the daunting prospect of legal battles, the soul-bruising skepticism that greets your lived truth, and the incessant reliving of your trauma, making you feel re-victimized by the very process meant to bring justice.

Offering advice to fellow survivors is a task fraught with complexity because the path forward is neither clear nor gentle, and each journey is deeply personal. What's unequivocal, though, is that the choice—to speak or to keep silent—carries profound consequences. Each survivor must weigh these outcomes within the context of their own resilience, support systems, and emotional landscape. This decision is arguably one of the most monumental they will face, as it doesn't just concern the aftermath of their trauma—it's about reclaiming agency, seeking justice, and embarking on the healing process, knowing there's no route devoid of pain, just paths strewn with different challenges.

If you need a confidant you will find me at triano.com

> *"We never truly vanquish our inner shadows; instead, we learn to rise above them."*
>
> —Melissa Triano

A Tribute to My Uncle Gary

In Her Wink: A Mother's Legacy

When shall we learn to greet life with a wink,
To find in a smile a world linked?
A woman I know guides the globe with grace,
Whose absence leaves giants yearning for her embrace.

Her laughter, a balm for all that's awry,
Sings through the air, a perpetual lullaby.
A charm from her being, in waves, does emit,
Blessing those near her with the warmth of her spirit.

Her intent is not whimsy, but a crafted art,
To dissolve the barriers that keep us apart.

Near her, a stranger one cannot remain,
She draws out your joy and alleviates your pain.
Challenge her with sorrow, she'll reverse the reel,
Her guileless spirit makes the unreal, real.

Her example is simple: be kind, be bold,
For niceness is a treasure better than gold.
Strength alone can demand too high a toll,
For the heart's conquest must start from the soul.

Her influence is not to command or to steer,
But to brighten the world, to hold this moment dear.
So we may revel, even if time were to freeze,
In the now that is ours, with the greatest of ease.

The gift of life has graced me, I confess,
With a marvel whose guidance is boundless.
Should I follow her lead, live true and just,
Echoing her, a compliment that would be robust:

"You mirror her essence," they'd say with delight,
A tribute to my Mother, my beacon so bright."

—**Inspired Through Love, by Gary Lee Triano**
who started this poem for my Grandma Toni,
before he died and I tweaked it!

About the Author

Melissa Triano, a native of Tucson, Arizona, has led a life as vibrant and varied as the landscapes of her hometown. Her adventurous spirit has taken her on an extraordinary journey around the globe, having sailed the seven seas and explored the rich cultures of 52 different countries. These experiences have not only broadened her worldview but have also deeply enriched her understanding of the myriad ways in which people live and thrive.

Throughout her career, Melissa has been a stalwart figure in the real estate industry, where her expertise and genuine empathy have set her apart. Her professional endeavors, however, represent only one facet of her multifaceted life. Since 2016, Melissa has been a national speaker for RAINN (Rape, Abuse & Incest National Network), playing a pivotal role in the powerful "Won't Stay Quiet " campaign.

Driven by a profound commitment to helping others, Melissa focuses her efforts on aiding those battling post-traumatic stress and preventing suicide. Her advocacy work is informed by her own experiences and her deep-seated desire to offer hope and assistance to those struggling to overcome traumatic experiences. Melissa's approach is one of empathy, understanding, and unwavering support, as she strives to illuminate a path to healing and resilience for many.

About the Author